Going to swim
over the seven seas

DAI MORISHITA
21-years-old resume

Seikosha

Keep Moving ～ Going to Swim Over the seven seas ～

Copyright © Dai Morishita 2016.
by Seikosha Co.,Ltd.
All rights reserved. Printed in Japan. First edition of Japanese,2012.
Book designed by Noriko Hayashi.
Printed by International Printing Publishing Laboratory Co., Ltd.

ISBN978-4-86372-084-8

The Seven Seas

Seas on the earth are defined that Ocean(the Pacific Ocean,the Atlantic Ocean and the Indian Ocean) and other seas.

There are two types of other seas, One is Mediterranean sea like the Mediterranean, and the Red sea which are between the Arabian peninsula and Africa.
The other is Coast like the Japan sea and Arabian sea which are devided by peninsula from oceans.

There is no clear definition of the seven seas by any laws, and may change which seas are the seven seas time to time.

In general, Going to the seven seas means going to seas all around the world.

Want to do.

Get a job what I like,
Get satisfaction through my job,
Live with my sweetheart
           with some money,
    I will be so happy !

      Be interested in many things,
         and Try them,
            It is good enough.
                   I believe so.

★ INDEX ★

Birth of a earth man 9

Coming back to Japan !! 33

Ibaraki East Junior High School days 39

Settsu High School days 55

Going to University of the Ryukyu 79

Start new Life in Okinawa 91

Activities in the University COOP 111

Many friends In Okinawa 124

Soccer Foot Ball Liverani 132

Surf Ball 135

Umi bu 143

Water Rock Rugby 153

Life Saving 165

Archaeology	195
Maritime Archaeology	205
Going to Australia	223
Back to Japan	269
Resume	287
Special thanks!!	299

Maru as the Morishita Family

Her Name is Maru naming from Naruto Caturn.
How cute she is!! (#^ ^#)

1 Birth of a earth man

Dai Morishita

Gender　　　　Male

Birth day　　　22nd February 1989

Birth of Place　Cardiff　South Glamorgan U.K.

Nationality　　The Earth

Hobby　　　　Swimming

Hi I am Dai Morishita.
I am a student of University of the Ryukyu.
I am learning Archaeology in the university.
Especially Maritime Archaeology which is not so popular.
I am just beginner of maritime Archaeology.
In addition, I am doing a lot of things which are interested for me but, may not be popular in general.

So I will introduce what I am doing now.
The story when I was born will be started.

So it is my pleasure if you may find something new.
Shall I start now so please read as you like.

Omiya Mairi (which is traditional event in Japan for praying health and happiness for a new baby born) at the LLandaff Cathedral near my home in Cardiff.

My friends say you are typical Osaka guy due to my osaka dialect.
But to be honest with you I was born in U.K.

I have been moving with my family due to my father's work assignment in overseas such as UK, Japan, Malaysia, and Japan something like this.

My nationality is Japanese but I feel I am a earthman.
Once becoming a friend, it does not matter with nationality, and everyone is just a human,
I would like to be as I am.

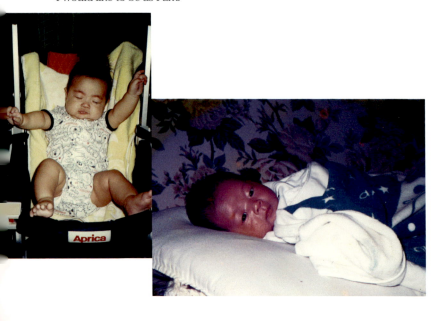

At 12 Southcourt Road
Pen-y-Lan Cardiff

1 Birth of a earth man

My brother Ryota is 3 years elder than me, he was born in Japan, I was born in UK. My mother must have a big job because of delivering me in overseas.

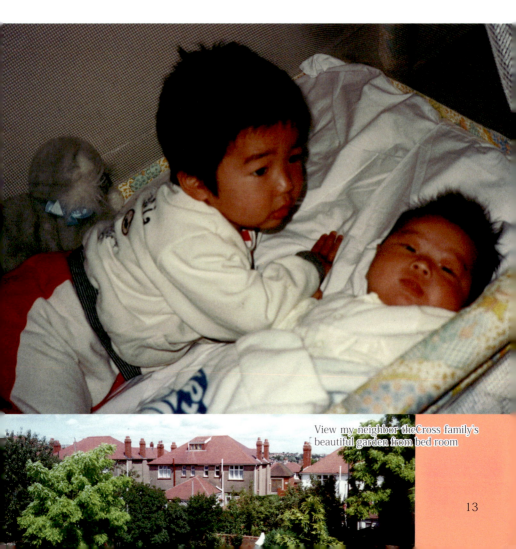

View my neighbor theCross family's beautiful garden from bed room

My sweet family

Playing a swing at garden with my father

My father, He is handsome!? used to be playing Rugby in his younger days.
He is great for working hard every day.

My mother is so sweet to me, She has never scold me in my memory.

I really thank to my parents since I am here.

at Majorca Island Spain July 1990

My first coming Back to Japan,Ceremony of Okuizome(Weaning ceremony) at my mothers' parents house at Hanozono cho Osaka in June 1989

1 Birth of a earth man

Ryota is genius,
I thought I also become genius,
when I have passed the University.

    Kumi My younger sister.
    She is so cute,
    She choose same high school and
    university as mine.
    She is quite right!

Visiting HMS victory at Portsmouth with Yuki & his mother

Oh I am so cute! I have to praise myself.

Wales where I have been until I was 3years old is very beautiful place.

There is a border with England on its eastern side, and it has many historical places.

Three national parks, five national reservation districts.

There are mountains and seas within about 170 miles from north to South, and 60 miles from east to west.

Cardiff is the Capital of Wales and biggest city in Wales.

Max and Samantha kindly came and gave special X'mas Presents for Ryota and Dai on 24th Dec 1991.

Southcourt Road In front of my house

I entered the Roath Park Kindergarten Nursery in April 1991 at Cardiff.

Nursery is children room let's say like Hoikuen in Japanese.

Hideki and myself are only Japanese within the nursery.

I heard that I am very popular and sweet wearing Welsh Rugby Jersey.

Maybe only My father says like this.

Great honor wearing Wales Jersey with red Sock of Am-pan man!

3 years Birthday party at Pent wyn Leisure Centre with friends 22nd Feb 1992.

Sleeping during my mothers' shopping May 1991

Made a Snow man with Yuriko and Ryota at Yuriko's garden in Lakeside Cardiff Feb 1991,Snowing is seldom occasion.

Kumi was born!!

Kumi my younger sister was born in Jan 1994 ♪

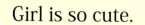

Girl is so cute.

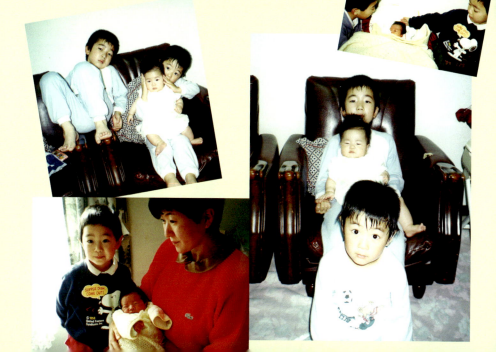

Can see my apartment on the 6th Floor Kiara Park

I have been living at Kuala Lumpur in Malaysia from 5 years old until 10 years old. There are swimming pools at the apartment.

This Pool might be the origin led me to the water.
There is no way to talk about me without water!

It must be a opportunity which given by my parents, Thank you.!

Relaxing at the Pools of the condominium Kira Park

Dancing with friends wearing Malaysian local clothes at the Japanese Kindergarten.
6th from the right is me.

With my father's friend Ramesan's children in KL

I have been enjoying at the kindergarten.
Then after going to enter the Japanese Elementary school at Kuala Lumpur, so called JSKL.

Shying with friends at the Japanese Kindergarten 18th Jan 1995

At Kindergarten class room 15th Nov 1994

At the entrance ceremony of Japanese Elementary School of K.L. with Ryota

Keeping a good boy at the class room after the ceremony.

1 Birth of a earth man

The Total Solar Eclipse

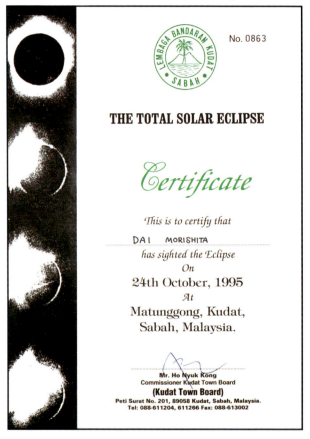

My father decided to go to Cota kina balu at the borneo Island to observe the total solar eclipse on 24th Oct 1995.
So this is the certificate for members who joined the tour.

Like this,I got chances to visit many places and events taken by my parents in Egypt, Spain and Italy so on.
Having interest in the history must be a influence from my parents.

I am very shy to show my essays for 3 years on the Rajah Brook which published by The Japanese Elementary School of KL.

There are big gap between this and the thesis for examination for the university and Graduation.

How much I improved!

Rajah Brooke

from the Rajah Brooke of JSKL

《1st grade》

Title: Went to the sea　Dai Morishita

I went to the sea on 23rd Oct.
There are many fishes in the sea,and my brother jumped into the sea when he found a lot of fishes in the sea.
But when he jumped into the sea,could not find the fishes anymore.
Then after my brother has been attacked by jerry fish!
When We moved to the next island,My dad found more fishes over there.
I came to my dad and found a lot of fishes there.And my mum found more fishes

《2nd Grade》

Title: Making the Base Camp   Dai Morishita

I had a chance to make a base camp on 1st Nov.
I choose to make a horror house.
Members are Saito, Okubo, Reo, Mizumoto and myself.
How to make horror house, we separated into two groups, one is making
Tunnel, and the other is making the building like a house.
At first made a mask and hung it up in the house,
Then after two more masks were made and make freighten when someone
come in the house.
We are visiting other base camp on 4th lesson
The first one is horror hotel, There are sword in the house, then after went
into the horror house, There were mens room and womens room in the house,
it seemed interested. After Coming back to our base camp, it slightly damaged,
but I really enjoyed it.

Title: The Athletics meeting   Dai Morishita

The athletic meeting was held on 22nd June.
I was getting nervous just after starting it,but getting well soon after.
The first race is hurdle race by 3rd grade.

《3rd Grade》

I am not good at first in the morning,I did not have energy but soon got the
energy.
The race was started, First hurdle was cleared well,but I had against on the
next one.
The after next,I could jump over successfully,and could goal in a top group.
Then after 5th and 2nd grade dance were finished.
The sirat was started by 3rd and 4th grade.
I have got nervous again,,but getting better during doing sirat.
I drunk a juice since I felt tired.
My dad is my next,and could see my brother further.
Rope game's results was not sure.
Anyway I really enjoyed the athletic Meeting.

At 3rd Pesta Subang

Act as Fox at the Pesta Subang of Japanese School of Kuala Lumpur(JSKL)

At Taman tun Park near my house Kiara Park

Swing at Kiara Park

Nice in Hot weather at Kira Park

Climbing up Jungle gym at JSKL

at Crocodile Land in Singapore Dec 1995

at Ryota's 9 years birthday party on 19th Nov 1995

With Ryota at Taman Utama Park

With Ryota at Clarke Quay in Singapore Dec 1995
Sliding down on the bar at Staircase

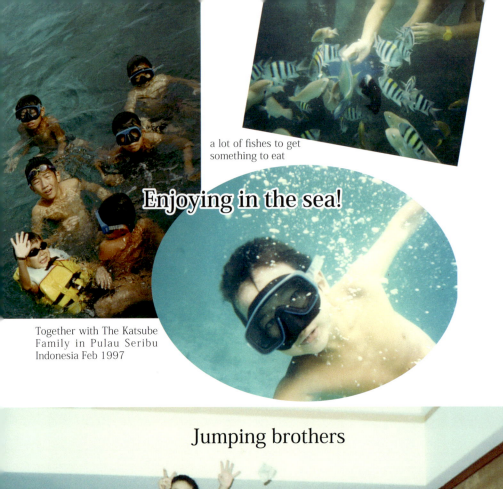

a lot of fishes to get something to eat

Enjoying in the sea!

Together with The Katsube Family in Pulau Seribu Indonesia Feb 1997

Jumping brothers

Hugging a Kangaroo as my first visit to Australia at Perth Feb 1996

I want to be a Dad
who fill car's trunk
with activities goods.

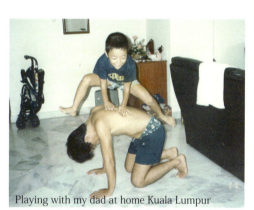
Playing with my dad at home Kuala Lumpur

Joining Dad's Get together at Port Dickson

To London from Malaysia

Halloween

Halloween party,,,
Bite with green face. →

At University's Halloween party ,,, remember child day's Halloween.

My face colored in Green. It seems that 3 years child soul may keep until 100 years olds
which is Japanese proverb,something like the proverb in English
'The leopard cannot change his spots'

Coming back to Japan !!
Joining into Ibaraki Municipal Oike Elementary School

Coming back to Japan !!

Playing everyday
in my elementary school days.

Playing Poke mon is
so exciting.

With Kaoru at execersion

Leaving the nest with smiling at
Graduation Ceremony of Oike
Elementary School
March 2001

With Grandmother at Kampo no Yado in Ako Hyogo Prefecture 11th Aug 1999

Relaxing on the Futon before going to sleep wih Ryota and Kumi at Kampo no Yado

Grandpa and Grandma of my mother at their home

Get together all of my mother's family at home

Coming back to Japan !!

Celebrating my mother's birthday at Hoken Centre in Senri Osaka on 8th Aug 1999

37

Hyaku nin Issu
(Traditional Japanese Tramp Card - One Hundred poems by 100 poets)

Learned Hyakunin-Isshu at 6th Grade of the elementary school.

Played Hyakunin- Isshu a lot at Morishita Family.

Since Do not want to be beaten by my elder brother,I have got a card which I can get without loosing.

It is
Momoshiki ya
furuki noki ha no
shinobu nimo
nao amariaru
mukashi narikeri
　　　Jun-toku in.

That is the 100th ' card of Hyaku nin- issshu
It means that
It was so good with remembering prosperity with viewing of grasses on the old houses

Ibaraki East Junior High School days

Standing in front of the main Gate at the opening Ceremony of the Ibaraki East Junior High School 9th April 2001.

Ibaraki East Junior High School days

Left is Macho

Macho

I have been together with Macho from elementary school until high school.
So such long period with him.
He is my first friend giving a word to me when I was hesitating to get a friend since just transferred from Malaysia.

Swimming club at Gacchu

Wataru,Kohei,Kachan, and me, four of us made a relay team at the swimming club. We decided own part appropriately so that I was in charge of butterfly.

We won the 3rd prize at the match of Ibaraki citizen cup.

Butterfly is really tough.

At first Kohei said I do breaststroke, then after we decided by toss,somehow I have been doing butterfly since then.

We have been keeping good team work and good friends for a long time.

Ibaraki East Junior High School days

Certificate of commendation

3rd Prize 200 m mens relay for 1st grade junior high.
Ibaraki East junior high school
Suzuki,Morishita,Matsumoto and Konishi

2min 35.00 seconds

You have got the above prize at the competition of Swimming in Spring organized
By Ibaraki & Mishima Pubulic Junior High School Athletics Federation.

17th June 2001

Makio Kobayashi
Chairman
Ibaraki & Mishima Public Junior High School Athletic Federation

Back stroke	Wataru Suzuki
Butterfly	Dai Morishita
Breast stroke	Kohei Matsumoto
Free style	Katsuya Konishi

Get together with my friends

My mother says,,,
It is very hard to get your time during your short staying back in Osaka since your schedule is always full with your friends in Osaka.
With my friends of Gacchu(at the Junior high school)and Settsu-ko(High school), so I am really busy with them during my staying Osaka.

Ibaraki East Junior High School days

Four of us after long time absence of my Staying Australia.

◇ Pieces of Memories ◇

☆ Let's draw a carton
Decision was made by four of us to draw a carton,but anyone could not complete,,,,

☆ Water boys
Tried imitated 'Water Boys' cinema when it was popular

☆ Cannon ball
Did imitated Cannon Ball! by doing white breath in winter season.

☆ Wasabi Nori
I were absorbed in Wasabi Nori(Seaweed with Wasabi spices)
Tried to eat it as much as together buying at Seven-eleven or sweet shops during Juku(evening sub-schools).My record is 5 pieces at once with tears,,

☆ Fukigen
It was Lactic acid bacteria carbonated beverages.
Often bought it when it gives cell phone Strap as Omake(Free gift)

Work Experience

I had a chance to get work experience with various type of works at my 2nd grade of junior high.
There were so many choices of works.

My job was goods keeper at Al-Plaza Heiwado Super Markets.
After working, I luckly got a side dish meals.

Some of my friends have got icecreams, some got dumplings, some went to Chinese restaurant, and nursery,,
It is so good memories, and good work experience for me.

School Trip

In front of the Fuji Television Office
School trip to Tokyo and Fuji mountain of Ibaraki East Junior High School
15th-17th May 2003

Ibaraki East Junior High School days

I was with Kohei in same room
during my school trip, but
Kohei fell asleep when I took a bath!
I can't believe it!!

Get together with kohei,macho ,,, In Sin-kan sen

School Festival

Mount. Fuji.

This is Harie (Pasting Picture with small pieces of paper) which shows Mount. Fuji at 2nd grade school festival.
This was Masterpiece!

When I was 1st grade, we drew up the Australia map as group activities, I was Incharge of painting the rock. That was rubbish!

Ibaraki East Junior High School days

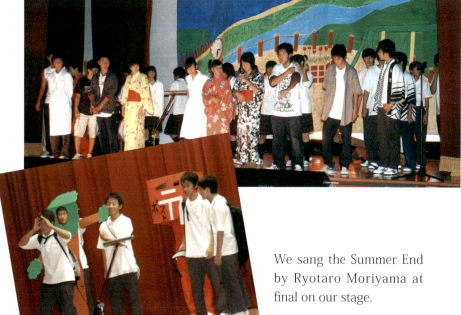

We sang the Summer End by Ryotaro Moriyama at final on our stage.

We played musical titled "Searching Summer Color" at the 3rd grade festival.

I acted a man of the village.

Even not main actor of this musical, I had a chance to say words.

We have got appraisal from PTA,even though other classmates did not appraised well!

Graduation Ceremony at the Junior High School

Inaba cho is great!!

Written On the album of the graduation.

The Swimming team on your left, Wataru, Kacchan, Kohei, and Dai

with Swimming club teacher and Miss Matsui.

★ I love Jibri ★

『 **Sen to Chihiro no Kami kakushi** 』
(Mysterious disappearance of Sen and Chihiro)
Love so much !!!!!!!

『 **Mimi wo sumaseba** 』 (if hearing carefully)
Bought a music box of 'COUNTRY ROAD' which is main song of its.

『 **Neko no On-gaeshi** 』 (Special thanks from Cats)
Went the cinema with Kohei and Kacchan.
I missed to watch the climax at the final of this movies, which is so famous
I could not bear my toilets......
So When I came back to my seat, already the screen showed the end role,,,
They shouted how good the climax is !
Mmmmm,,,

Settsu High School days

Osaka Prefectural Settsu High School
Very active for athletics club activities showing celebration flags for entitled to the inter high(all Japan High school competition) and competiton in Kinki(Kwansai district)

Main Gate of the high school

How sweet my school is!

Kumi also spent her school days there.

She loved running at the track & fields club.

She was popular with both Sports and Study.

with friends of tennis Club

My Tennis Club

I am not good at playing tennis since I have just started at my high school.

Some of my friends have improved their tennis even they were also beginner in high school.

I have been keen for practicing tennis even in the morning activities,,

with friends of tennis club at tennis coat

I used to make fun with my friends during waiting to play in the tennis court since only limited members can play in the court at the same time.
And often scold by teachers since imitated pant mime and practicing without taking clothes.

Be careful with 21st books of Hana yori Dango(Animation)

School excursion
Class 4 3rd grade to
Kobe as final in
high school days

Part time job

I have been working at Ohsho restaurant since my 2nd grade of high school with my friend Konya.

Because I wanted to get a motor bicycle, I have started to work there,

but I bought a motor bicycle first with borrowing money from my father, because it was so far to get the Ohsho restaurant from house.

It was so expensive which I wanted to get,

During my work in Osho, I have been in charge of washing dishes, so no chance to cook.

But I am good at cooking Tenshin han(Eggs rice).

Tenshin han of Osho is best in any where else!!!!!!

It came true of Horror Phenomena at Kimo dameshi
(Competition of Braves)

We had stolen into our school for Kimo Dameshi on our way back from some events of the school.

During walking through of the school building,It sounded Bohhnn,which like bounded tennis ball near by tennis court.

There should not be remained any tennis balls after our practicing since clear up the tennis court by members normally.

Oh Goshu,,,,,Everyone was freighten,,,and
I accidentally saw a man who wore white shirt, but no one wore white shirt on that day!!
There is a story later, A student who have throw balls on that day was shouted by himself
On the day of our graduation,,,
Anyway It was so scared,,but still mysterious of white shirt guy,,,,

Please permit our stolen into the school due to time over.

We often did fire works around the monuments or under the bridge,

Meet up with Okinawa
~So exciting school trip to Okinawa~

School trip, How good it was, everyone was so excited!

It was well prepared getting new clothes for the trip together with friends.

Hats are all the same within the class.

Looking those pictures again, it becomes shy.

It was so attractive with doing various kinds of marine sports for 4days at Miyako Island of Okinawa prefecture.

Especially it was marvelous for getting banana boats over Irabu Island!

The sea of Okinawa was perfect!,

It was the opportunity for me to be loved with Okinawa.maybe,,,

I can remember that it was so deep and cold under the sea when I swam to the open sea during waiting for banana boat's turn.

Our Class 7 won the hurley race since we did make our own tactics with good team works.
After the match we jumped into the sea with big pleasure.
Some of us were stung by jelly fish.
The final schedule was fishing,but it was cancelled and alternated to visit the botanical garden.

It was regrettable but everyone said if more excited by fishing,no one wish to be back to Osaka anymore.

We have got another fun by musical chairs.
One more surprise was birthday celebration for Mr.Yanagi during this trip, it was well arranged to imitate Makkin and Kiku chan fight each other.
The BGM songs were "Special Words" to you by Yuzu.
Our class often held birthday party with surprised.

We were excited to talk a lot of Bump of chicken, Mr.Children with makkin Kikuchan and Yanagi during art classes

the guide book of School trip to Okinawa

So excited Schedule for 21st June, 22nd June

It was so excited everyday!

I was really attacked by Okinawa's sea.

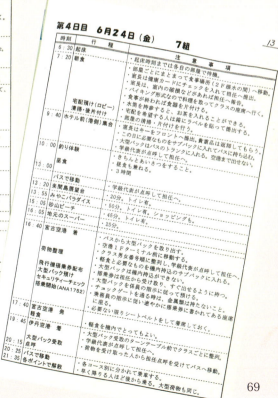

Continued schedule for 23rd June to 24th June.

at Classroom

Seven frame cartoon

Took photos for seven frame cartoon in the room during school trip. Yanagi, Ueda, Funo, Kikuchan, Hiroshi, makkin and I took one scene by each.

So no chance to be seven frame cartoon unless 7 of us get gathering with their camera.

It was showing at the back of class room for a while, but it was disappeared time to time.

Hope to see it again one day.

Wearing T shirt drawing up of brown sugar with Konya

Settu High School days

I was called
~DADAI~

I was called Da-Dai, since I heard often saying
   Dadas dai dadas(from Terminator)

Class 7 of 2nd Grade was
         so sweet and good team!

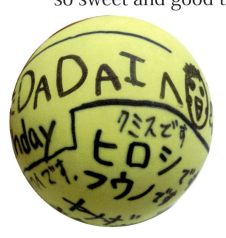

The presented tennis ball from friends on my birth day.
Signed by many of friends, but no one remember it.

Excited School Festival

Scenes from festival

Settsu high school has internal rules of activities for each grade at the school.
1st Grade Playing acts at Gymnasium
2nd Grade is taking food stand.
3rd grade is dancing

> Our Class (class 7 2nd grade) did a game centre named Nn-myachi Centre named from Okinawa dialect.

Meaning of Nn-myachi is Welcome in Miyako island,which is Men-sole in Okinawa Main island.

Dancing Matsu-ken Samba at School festival on 2nd Grade.

This is special T shirts of Class 7 for school festival.
Eeveryone has got their own name on the back, There was Doraemon above my name Dai somehow.

Dancing

With Dorae-mon

Settu High School days

Dancing O-nyanko Club between events just making fun!

Thanks for Making up
by Moritani

Thanks for Moritani taking care of me so much
When I went to Okinawa, She kindly game me a lot of tooth paste!
She is dental hygienist!!
In addition She kindly sent some food to me I really thank you.

Graduation trip to Kinosaki Onsen

(Hotspring Kino-saki in Hyogo Prefecture)

We went around Hot springs with Yanagi, It was so called Sotoyu Meguri (Tour of Hot spring)

After taking many hot springs, took a drink, gatrade finally at once.

It was so nice, since no drinks has been taking during our tours.

By the way, at that time, My direction to university has not been decided yet!!

So delicious famous Crub in Kinosaki

Playing game which named Wink-killer taught by me to everyone.

Various scenes at Settsu High School

Best 3 menu at canteen

- Chicken cutlet — 100 Yen
- Kara-age Deep flied Chicken — 50 Yen
- Indian flied rice and Curry — 50 Yen

Canteen of Settsu High School

Especially Chicken Cutlet was excellent with milk tea! It was so good, but seems no chance to get any more due to the changes of canteen's owner.

Mountain Dew

Red bull Good for encouraging ourselves in School festival.

Kokyu chocolate called God chocolate since so good almost like god! I love with blue one.

Shiso(Perilla) Juice which hand made by my mum is best in the summer time.

Gokuraku Yu(Hot Spring) in Ibaraki and members Card

Members card of Gokuraku-yu is proven of the status!✌

Sweat of Lemonade by Shimada Often said Shimada to Miss Shimada too.

Going to University of the Ryukyus !!

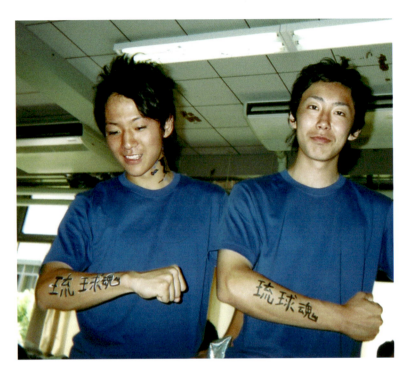

I have decided to go to University of the Ryukyus where is best place in my school trip and can learn Archaeology which is only few univeresity have cources.
Let's go to University of the Ryukyus!
So, I have to study first to pass the examination.

Going to University of the Ryukyus !!

The application form for the National and Public University

Please describe the reason to apply for following University,college,subject,specialty

Desiring University : University of the Ryukyus
Desiring College,subject,and specialty:
The Faculty of Law and Literature human Science course Geography & Anthropology.

I wish to learn history in the university, since I was interested in history when I was in junior high school.
Especially, I became to have much interest in the Archaeology in my high school.
And interested in remains and world heritage site too.
At that time I met a book which is regarding with submarines remains,I have become to have more interest in Okinawa's remains since not only submarines remains but also other remains in Okinawa with reading through the book.
And I found that university of the Ryukyu has got the course of Anthropology from University Information. More I study more enthusiasm come on me.
I have been impressed with the view and scales of the university's campus.
I could not stop my energy wishing to go to University of the Ryukyu with beautiful sea and nature which is far better than Osaka's
And I have learned how interest and difficult Anthropology is,with hearing from the explanation of the course of Anthropology there.

In addition with this, another reason why I wish to go to university of the Ryuku is that there are so many subject of selection.
I thought that it is so attractive for students to choose subjects depending on their interest and needs from over 270 subjects.
I heard that I can learn various type of subjects such as like Okinawa's own culture to the Asian and European Cultures.
It is quite far from Osaka, so I may have some difficulties, but I am confident to spend good university life through 4 years.
That is the reason why I apply to University of the Ryukyu.

37 Class 4 3rd Grade Settsu High School Osaka Dai Morishita

81

Rose WAM is our origin

I believe, that no chance to pass the examination, if not study at Rose WAM.

I have studied there every day except on Tuesday when it is closing.

I loved to drink bean milk flavored with banana taste paper packed on automatic vender machine.

At Mocchan Tako yaki shop

Tako yaki with soap mayyonaisse by Mocchan is best

> Note
> Review of 1st term on 3rd Grade
> I recognized that I was too optimistic to pass to desired university ,and need to effort a lot!
> So I will do my best with smiling!!

View of the building of Rose WAM(Note*1) (Note*1-WAM is Women and Men collaboration Centre by Ibaraki City council)

as above

As for the memories at Rose WAM, I have asked a girl who was sitting next to me to give a piece of her gummy candy so sudden without considering anything!
She kindly gave me a gummy candy,,,,,,
How shy I am since I never know her at all!
My friends sitting with me could not stop laughing so much!

I am missing the time when I was going to e-seminal at Ibaraki.

Exam. Study for the University

I have been desiring to do something related with history, since I was interested.
I wanted to study Archeology.
Archeology is very mysterious.
There are not so many Universities where I can learn Archeology.
University of Nara,Kyoto Tachibana University and university of the Ryukyu,,,
I have decided to get the examination for these 3 universities.
University of the Ryukyu is best for me, since located in Okinawa where my favorite place near to the sea, and one of the National university!

Since National university,it is necessary to take Common Centre Examination by ministry of the education.
I have been studying mathematics so hard.
As for English,I had no idea how to study it!
In addition with this, short thesis, short thesis?! What is thesis?
How tough for me to write sentences.
I have started to drop down to the teachers room around at the end of 2nd term 3rd grade.
I asked my class teacher and other teachers to teach me on my poor thesis.

Going to University of the Ryukyus !!

When I showed my thesis to my class teacher at the first time,
She asked me that Have you ever written any sentence, Morishita ?
So to be honest, I was so poor on writing.

My teacher guided me to describe ki-sho-ten-ketsu(Scenario of Thesis comes from 4 steps like introduction,Own Opinion,issue to be and goal with showing a word on each box on folding B4 sized paper and directed me to describe a sentence by each box.
In fact It really teaching hand to hand.
As such I had tough times, wondered how many times I went to teachers' room,even I have caught other teachers there to learn.
I guessed teachers were not expected me to pass the examination since too late to start.
At the end,I have kept learning from them until after my graduation ceremony of the high school,just before the examination at around in March with their kind guidance.
They have been kindly taking care of me until the final minute.
My direction has not been decided at the time when I have travelled with my friends as graduation trip.
I did what I could do! it is enthusiasm!

> I missed the chance to get the examination for the Kyoto Tachibana University since Just forgetting the date.
> It was so funny to remember.
> My mother also just kept smiling with me.

Open Campus

I went to the open Campus of university of the Ryukyu after my decision to get examination.
With My friend, Kohei Suzuki who also wishes to go there.
University of the Ryukyu was so good!! Since We have got a lot of learning from senior of the university as support team for candidates.

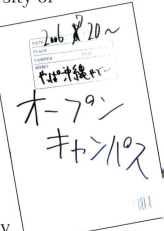

my daily of Open campus on 20th July 2006 Okinawa is best!

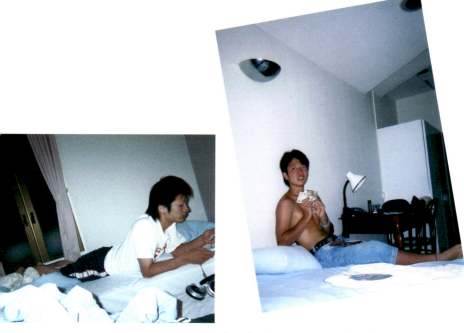

The hotel where we stayed with Hohei Suzuki seams lovers' hotel in the past.

Support for candidates by seniors

I went to the examination for university of the Ryukyu with Eguchi.
Encouraged so much!

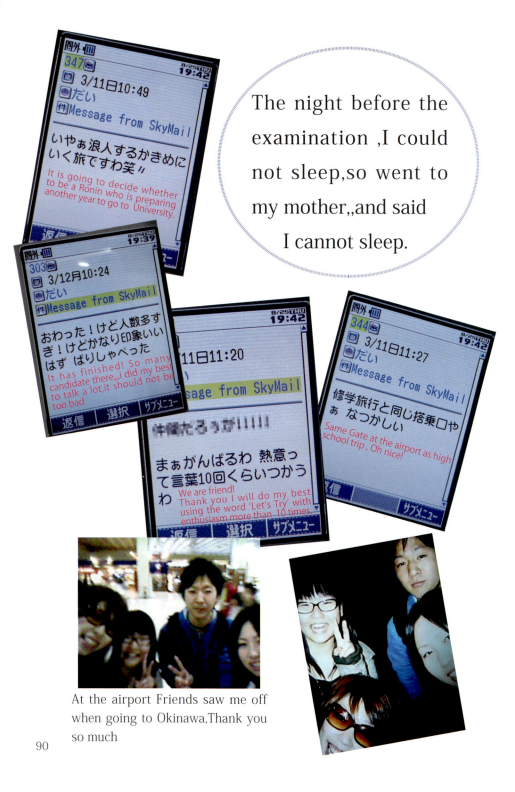

Start new life
in Okinawa

the Entrance Ceremony!

I came to Okinawa on 3rd April,and following day, on 4th held a welcome party for us.
I was a staff of welcome party, started to prepare it from 1 o'clock in the afternoon.
To be ready for 7 o'clock.
It was rather hard, but really enjoyed it!

On following day, so I woke up around 12 o'clock afternoon even the ceremony started 9 o'clock in the morning.
I was embarrassed so much, but when I called my friend, he has also slept over, too.
It made me happy
Even we were late, everything was all right,
How good the university is! It is not so severe.

My new life in Okinawa

On 12th April 2007
How big the university is! It really vaste!
I am going to register my classes.!
And also I have got a lot of new friends already!
I did not have enough time for sleeping since so many activities such as welcome party for new comers, trial experience for new circle especially in night.

Oh,I had got a promise with my senior to have a chance to watch stars in the night!
How smart University students' activities are !
I am becoming exciting since Stars in night at Okinawa seams so great!

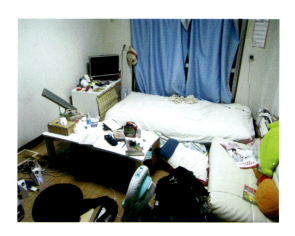

Do part time job!

15th Apr 2007

The class will be starting tomorrow,it seams so late.

Anyway Do my best for various things.

Now, my Osaka Dialect become strange!!

Living by myself!

Today sprout became bad.

I felt that living by myself is troublesome at the first time.

It smell so bad once sprout became bad!

Kimuchi(Korean pickled cabbage),yogurt also expired the date for eating.

In my refrigerator, there are only eggs, cheese,mayonnaise and tomato ketchup only which can be eaten.

My frying pan is not good at all,since it was only 500JPY with three in one.

Handle becomes so hot when I do cooking by using it.

What can I do ?

Tomorrow I will get a motor cycle so that I can go anywhere.

This is a motor cycle owned by Hiroshi.

Start new life in Okinawa

Swimming & circle activities!

I will go to get a swim wear after classes today.

In my university life, I will do club and circle activities as much as I can.

Swimming Club.Tennis Club and Diving Circle!

There are big difference between Ryukyu's swimming club and others.

Playing rugby in the sea so called Water rock rugby is also doing.

How good they are Number one in Japan!

I also will be the number one in Japan too.

As for tennis club, practicing once a week. But my friend is representative of
Shizuoka Prefecture in his high school. He is inter-high player!
Diving needs money first,, to do it need to get its lisence too. It seems to tired.

Fire extinguisher!!

How troublesome after using fire extinguisher !

It was really lucky for vanishing fire by using fire extinguisher,but It is better not to have such experience to use it.

Oh dear,,,,,It is really pity,,

The situation after using fire extinguisher for vanishing fire grilled fishes.

Start new life in Okinawa

Live by myself   Part 2

I love egg so much.
So when I open my refrigerator, I found already 10 days has gone after expiring the date for eating.
Yesterday I have eaten fried egg!
Just now I found.
Not only egg, but also Milk, yogurt are also expired ! Ooh,,,,,,,
Few days ago, I made pan cake by using those eggs, milk.
Oh dear,,,,
I want tenshin han (Chinese egg omelette rice) of Ohsho.
Oh-sho is not in Okinawa yet, even nobody know Oh-sho.
In addition, Bikkuri Ramen and Seven eleven are not in Okinawa either.
I do not see Sai zeria here,,

Instead, here it makes me big surprise!!
Serving volume is almost double!

Washing dishes is more troublesome for me rather than cooking.
If I make a lot, it makes me regret later for eating up them.
So recently I normally make a one dish, 80% cases are fried rice.

Oh-sho Tenshin han
One more Tenshin han
Oh-sho fried rice

Encounter with Awful thing

31st July 2007 02:18

I have spent good day with reporting in the morning, circle activities in the daytime and
In the evening I did part time job,
Just now I came back from my part time job, and found the bamboo door was open in my room.

I thought, Oh I forget to close it then after
I tried to take off my contact lenses for studying for tomorrow's examination.
At that time I encountered him under the switch of Toilet,

He is a cockroach !

he is really awful and big with brown colored.

Right now, I am still facing him.

If it is outside, it is no problem I can kill him !

But since here, in my room, in case I may crush him,his blood serum will be spread out to the wall!
How pity it is, keep opening bamboo door makes such a tragedy

It is no chance to talk about the examination.

I can escape to the Mac to continue my study, It makes them growth!

I guess the reason why I hesitate killing him is make dirty on my wall, but in fact,,,

I cannot wipe out of fear of flying cockroach during my club activities.

It was far better since outside and together with my fellows.

Here, closed space in the room and only myself!

It is almost end.
My room is under controlled by cockroach.
Recently I always eat Natto, so that cockroach are coming my room.
Dishes to be washed remain a lot now!
Cockroach disclose what I should improve!
I should say thank for cockroach in a sense.
Anyway I should take some actions for preparing my examination,
One idea is escaping to Mac' Donald, or crash out after falling down from the wall.

Maybe I will be attacked by cockroach at the time fall from the wall.

It is terrible!
Oh Gooosh!
He watches me!!

Oh, gooossh,

Kill him!

Alien Jones,,

Start new life in Okinawa

Typhoon in Okinawa is so dangerous.

Motor cycle does not work on typhoon day.

Winds makes motor cycle change the lane naturally.

雨降ってきた！

It is starting raining.

Hives make me annoyed.

It is long time since I had hives in my elementary school day.
I could not join crab party due to hives.
Oh dear,,,

No chance to study Spanish language either,but the examination was easy enough for me.
It must be more than 80 points.
I will visit to Miyazaki for swimming match tomorrow for 4days 3 nights.
Now we are practicing it dancing as entertainment after matches.
Unexpectedly It is same Algorithm Ozma in our dance as which I did at my high school.
So I do not have to practice much, but clothes are all ladies under wears, Oh dear!

Reception by Fukuoka where next years venue after Miyazaki.

This is at university festival at Ryukyu, my usual activities.

Start new life in Okinawa

Went to the swimming competition at Miyazaki on 10th 11th June. Beside matches, It was so exciting reception after the match.

Ryudai was best for enjoying dancing with ladies wears.

The swimming match of Public University in Kyushu!!　Kuhaaa!!

I have entried. 100m butterfly, 50m free and relay so on.

Hi,I still continue to swim butterfly, to my friends of Gacchu Swimming club!

Since choosing butterfly accidentally.

At that time,my butterfly life has been started there,,,

Oh,

Camp at Nakijin

Start new life in Okinawa

At Miyazaki for 2007 the competition match of Public University in Kyushu

Sep 2008 taking over Management team of Swimming club

Note of Management team Swimming Club Dai Morishita

10th May 2009
The Memorial of Wakakusa National Athletic Meet Swimming match
At Okinawa general athletic park

2009/5/10
平成21年度　若夏国体記念水泳競技大会
（沖縄県総合運動公園プール）

男子　50m　自由形
タイム決勝

順位	氏　名	所属	学年	記録	組	コース		備考
18	森下　大	琉球大	大学3	28.35	19	2	R	
20	千田　皓雪	琉球大	大学2	28.56	18	3	R	
31	岩本　哲尚	琉球大	大学3	29.76	18	1	R	
38	阿部　翔	琉球大	大学1	30.77	17	6	R	
50	喜瀬　大輔	琉球大	大学4	31.70	16	2	R	
64	林　洋平	琉球大	大学2	32.76	13	4	R	
棄権	嘉陽　宗史	琉球大	大学2		10	2	R	

男子　100m　バタフライ
タイム決勝

順位	氏　名	所属	学年	記録	組	コース		備考
10	小部　敬純	琉球大	大学2	1:12.11	2	5	R	
11	森下　大	琉球大	大学3	1:12.85	2	4	R	

Men's 50m free 18th Dai Morishita 28.35 Sec.,,,
Men's 100m butterfly 11th Dai Morishita 1:12.85 Sec.,,It seems nice records!

> Dai Morishita
> 50m free   28.35
> 100m butterfly   1.12.50

Start new life in Okinawa

Cape Kyan as Southernmost tip at Okinawa main island

Yesterday, the event so called Tanabata Drive was held by smimming club.
Went to the Cape Kyan where the southernmost tip at Okinawa Main island.
It was great! So many stars in the sky!!!!
I could see the milky way so clearly.
It is really perfect, no way,
Stars covered all the sky, There is no word to talk about!

Then after went to Kara OK, as everybody knows I am not good at singing.
But, from 2 o'clock mid night until 10 o'clock in the morning. Really tired,
So slept over in the daytime.
Went to Kokusai dori with Taichi & Hiroshi, enjoyed again!

Singing Karaoke,,it is really tough for me,,

Like U-chi nan chu
(behave like as native Okinawa)

26th June 2008 15:44 Shini(Really) raining,
so cannot go to swimming club although
The match is coming soon,it becomes trouble!

And, have a pain on my foot injured at Beach party, It is no way, all finished,
Shina suna yo!

Okinawa Dialect is really difficult for me,but love it since so cute,,,

Thanks for 100yen noodle shop especially Izutsu ya
It so convenient to drop-by there after drinking in the early morning since Opening at 3 o'clock in the morning ♪

Nada So so (Tear tear)

I watched a movie Nada so so, it is really impressive.
Well caught Okinawa, is it,

It is same classroom where I took the class Museum introduction as shown in the movie Masami Nagasawa was sitting.

It's really impressive.

Wanted to sit the same seat as she sat.

Shiee-sa(Statue of Okinawa lion)

When getting confused with so many things,it is good idea to do cleaning in the room, My high school teacher said that

So I do so
if confused in my head \(^o^)/

In Kenji's room

Ichariba*

Friend is so great.
Carro san's is eco activities started occasionally.
Through activities got firm friendship,satisfaction.
And did a lot
So nice to be there where I can meet a lot of friends.

*Ichariva : Activities of COOP at University of the Ryukyu

Ichariba Activities of COOP at University of the Ryukyu

As I talked I had got support from my seniors, when I came to the open campus, those students who supported me are committee of COOP. So called Ichariba.

Ichariba means that Once meeting each other, they will become brother and sister.

Activities of Ichariba are introduction of apartment, insurance, support many things for new comers.

So many activities are doing by Ichariba like Jyu-sapo, which means support applicants for the university, support freshman, open campus, bus hike, christmas party, so on ,,,

Members of committee is organized by students from various faculties and departments, In 2007 when I entered 22 members in 1st grade, 9 in 2nd 11 in 3rd, in addition with this, 4th grade and after graduated members are also supporting

On the day before the Entrance ceremony, Hai sai Party(Welcome Party) is held by Support centre for new college life every year.

At Hai sai Party, there are so called Freshmen who are selected from freshmen and prepare the party so that they can make friends before starting college life.

Ichariba activities At the Campus

Ichariba Activities of COOP at University of the Ryukyu

Somehow I was also selected to Freshmen.

The criteria for selection at that year was Cute for women, funny for men I heard,, why?

My senior when He took care of me at open campus took a lead on the party.

This occasion made memorial milestone for me to meet many friends in my college life.

I really thank to my senior who took me to Ichariva.

Advantage of Ichariba activities is getting a lot of friends

Friends is my treasure

Really thanks for meeting

Ichariba members

Waiting Applicants for guide at Naha Airport

Hai sai Party (Welcome Party)

Enjoyed with making Questions related with local city.
Since I am from Osaka,did like Question,,
「What is 551?」
「Oh Nobody know?」
Only students from Osaka know it and they enjoyed it.
Yes I am representative of Osaka,

Did Comte with Hiroshi

Oh yes,
Did practice a lot overnight for freshmen.
We were so keen!

We are Jin-ka!!
(Human Science course)

We went to the Loisir Hotel in Naha wearing smart suit for lunch!

Hi!

Events takes a lot of time from planning until finish it.

After class, we get together to make a plan and budget.

We have been busy until late night.

Someone say that Dai just keep looking after proposing a unique idea,,

No, in fact I am making sure milestones which would be important.

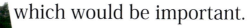

Cooling my head
cartoon says,,,seems get a flu!

Caro San's

Caro San's is a part of Ichariba especially for supporting environment.

Opening free market, and shop for Tako Sen(rice cake of Octopus) at "University of Enthusiasm".

Beach clean activities have been held 3 times titled with "Beach Clean at Tsuken Island".

All members Beach Clean at Zampa Maribu Beach.
(Tsuken Island 2 times, Mid-north area once)

many activities Ichariba Caro san's

Cannot enjoy now,
no chance to enjoy life.

If I sacrifice right now for the future,

the present time will not be happy.

There is no chance to enjoy future

without enjoying now.

Thanks for coming to my favorite Okinawa

Went around many places during their

staying in Okinawa and

really enjoyed!

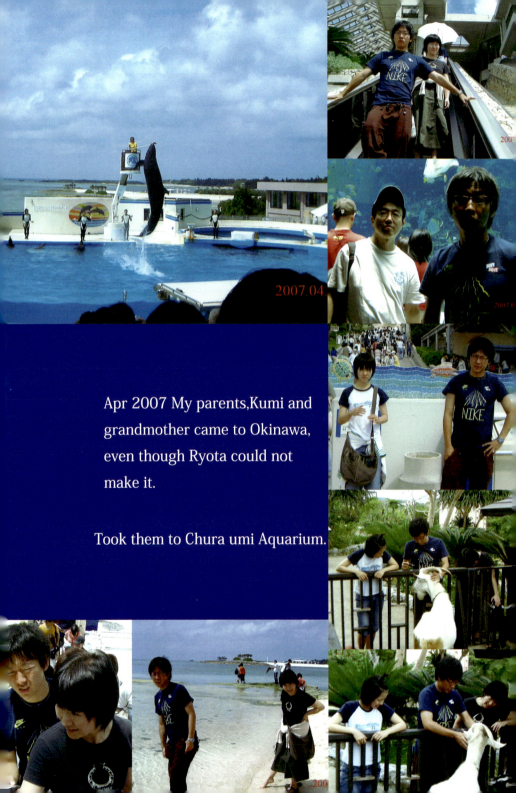

Apr 2007 My parents, Kumi and grandmother came to Okinawa, even though Ryota could not make it.

Took them to Chura umi Aquarium.

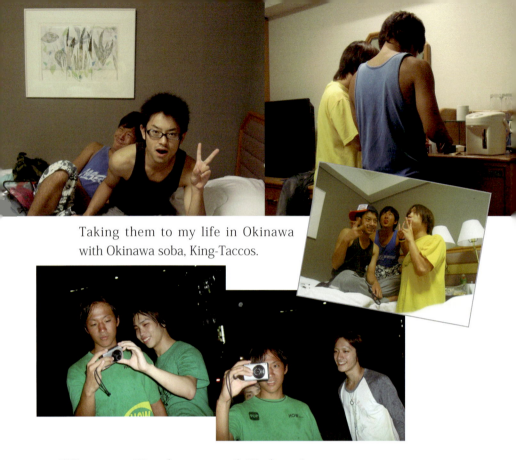

Taking them to my life in Okinawa with Okinawa soba, King-Taccos.

Wataru, Kachan, and Kohei !

Thanks for Swimming relay team coming over from Osaka.

Walking around the Kokusai Dori like tourists.

Thanks for all my friends visiting to Okinawa to see me!

Thanks for coming to my favorite Okinawa

Why not going to Chura umi Aquaium with Ryo

Thank you Ryo.

One of Best Awamori is Zam shiro (Zampa with white label)

With Ryota

Ryota also came to Okinawa!

Justaway ,my favorite!

Ryota my elder brother is stronger than me!

Thanks for coming to my favorite Okinawa

20 years old ceremony

Met my friends in Ibaraki , not so many changes anyway!

Some of them long time no see.

I feel at home now.

Exciting among with swimming club friends of Ibaraki Higashi JHS.

I am now 20 years old.

Morishita Family
in Vietnam!

Aug 2009 Visited Ho Chi Minh City in Vietnam with all my family Really enjoyed.

Liverani
Foot ball team

Even making team Uniform, I am not good member to join practices.

Surf Ball

Meet with Surf ball by 100,000 JPY !

Surf ball

How tough this sport is!

Running at the beach with friends even so hot in Okinakawa.

Really enjoyed when the team won, and regrettable when lost.

Even very tough, kept running at the beach.

A lot of practices have been done for winning of games,

Why can we do it?

Because team mates are there!

It is true why I could play it,since my team mates are there.

We cannot cheat friends each other,so everyone does his best.

It is surf ball

It is really occasion that we have got a flyer of Surf all competition when we walked around our university campus with friends.

A flyers says that

"Winner prize is 100,000 JPY.
Only for beginners, No specific condition to join."

So Hiroshi,Taichi and I were so excited and immediately to make a team gathering with guys who like playing sports.

Team names is Ryu-allies(ryu-Dragon,allies-alliance)

Surf Ball

A team work is most important on this sport, members of Ryu-allies made The Umi Bu (meaning Sea Club) later.

As for surf ball, it is like rugby and american foot ball at the beach.

We were confident to win since most of us have experience of various sports .

But it was not so easy to win, we were in 5th grade at the end.

We could not get 100,000JPY.

Surf ball is played by 5 players at each team, so even one of them not play well, It was easily loose score.

It is really tough to keep running for the team.

Although so tough, it is more than pleasure to play with team mates.

It is same to everyone,so we continue to run each other.

Very important to trust each other.it is same to as human.

It is impossible to keep a ball by oneself all the time, so we must make sure each player's position.

Communication is important between receivers and sender of ball to be stronger.

How good it is, If we won the game at that time,we might not be so enthusiastic with on surf ball.

We might think not necessary to practice more.

But we lost the game,did practices more to be stronger.

It is true that Ryu-allies and team mates are there.

Running all the time

for the team.

If could not do so,

cannot forget to be regretted.

With friends

Surf Ball !

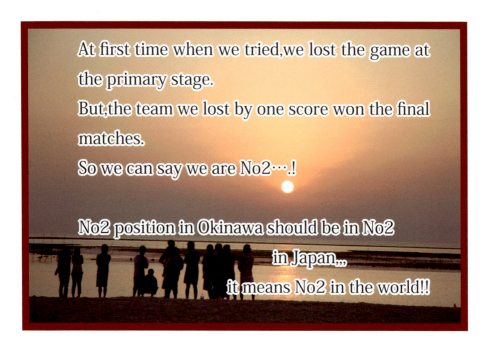

At first time when we tried,we lost the game at the primary stage.
But,the team we lost by one score won the final matches.
So we can say we are No2….!

No2 position in Okinawa should be in No2
in Japan,,,
it means No2 in the world!!

Dai is main player in Ryu-Allies,he always encourage team members saying like as above.
The Japan Surf Ball association thanks for his positive encouragement all the time and keep watching his activities.
The Ryu allies is No1 in their team works without any doubt

Shoei Okabe
The Japan Surf ball association.

Umi bu
(Sea Club)

Starting animation of diving from the wall

Umi bu

We have organized the Umi bu for playing all kinds of sports related with the sea since the lost of the surf ball matches.
For enjoying not only Swimming,but also all kinds of sports related with the sea.

We made a Welcome Board of the Umi bu at the newcomer welcome party.
It was so good!!

But the board is too big to show at the university campus.
So we put it at the front of the board of the student council.

Sorry of doing it,,the board tells that more than 100 members joined in the last year,,also telling a lie!

Anyway we are just playing the surf ball
and drinkings finally.

Umi bu (Sea Club)

Camp

Went the azama sun sun beach for our umi bu camping.
We tried to talk with tourist girls for getting captain's position.

1st day my team won,but only ate dinner with them
2nd day got together with island small boys.

Oh dear,,,,,

To do Nampa,tried to shout tourist girls to ask taking photos with saying that we are from southern area.

At the end,we have got so many photos showing same places and have been deleted at all.

We have not practiced surfball at all during Camp.

Something like this, we Umi bu always try to enjoy with drinking.

Oh,,,,

want to go to the sea!

「Let's drink ————!!!」

Charge

Before getting drunk, vomit first,,,

so that can drink continuously,,,

It so called Charge which

Is high level technics,,,

I am at the middle level,,

Kenji is
the GOD!

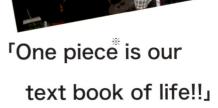

「One piece※ is our

text book of life!!」

※"One piece" is famous cartoon in Japan.

Love is best in the world!!

Famous place,,,
café Crewl at
Ganeko Ginowan
3-4-6 102

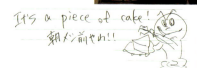

It is a piece of cake!
Meaning is that it is easy for me
like before breakfast,,,

Rock Rugby

Rock　I really want to see my friends of water rock rugby

Try to breath as long as I can

Need to muscle training

I do not want to be embarrassed…

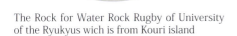

The Rock for Water Rock Rugby of University of the Ryukyus wich is from Kouri island

Yesterday, I met the sport so called Rock Rugby!!
It is amazing playing Rugby under the sea 3 meters below!
The ball is a rock weighted 34 KG!!
It is really attractive, a lot of fishes besides me,
Cramping many times
The sea is fully utilized!!

1st May 2007

Playing Water Rock Rugby,,,Try!

Water Rock Rugby

Rock Rugby was born in beautiful sea in Okinawa.

It has been created based on the training of big wavers or life guards in Hawaii for strengthen ning of Cardiopulmonary function.

It is playing under water around 3 to 4 meters and using 34KG weight stone instead of rugby ball.In a sense it is very unique under water sport!

Rock Rugby is so good for practicing swimming, diving ability, self defense ability(ability for avoid accident), and growing team work by training Rock rugby naturally.

The rule of Rock Rugby is very simple.

Goal is made by carrying a stone into opposite goal which is located in under water by two teams.

Water rock rugby is playing under water 100%, more goal makes team win.

It is impossible to make a goal by oneself since cannot manage without breath long time.

So Team work become important.

It seems difficult, but actually anyone who can swim can play it.

Once a year, the nationwide competition will be held in Okinawa gathering people who love the sea.

It is most welcome to play Rock Rugby, and watch the game.

Really wish many people trying to play it, so that can feel how good it is.

Rock Rugby players by Dai

Water Rock Rugby all Japan competition
Organized by All Japan Rock Rugby committee
info@owps.jp

The champion team LEGEND

Rock Rugby cannot be playing by oneself. It is not enough only with physical fitness, technique for making goal,

>It is more important to communicate each other by contacting each other's mind(stone).

♪ ROCK MY SOUL

ROCK MY SOUL
　Let's dive with everyone
ROCK MY SOUL
　Let's run with everyone
ROCK MY SOUL
　Let's connect with everyone
OH ROCK MY SOUL

Playing rock rugby under sea

We cannot talk each other playing rock rugby under the sea.
It is difficult to understand each other even on the land.

Important to find team mate who need breath looking around because even good player need breath.
Water Rock Rugby need the mind to understand team mate and confident each other .
So it is dangerous to play with someone who meet at the first time.
Participants are coming by team or individually from various places in Japan.
It may have a case to make a team so sudden.
So the completion of Water Rock Rugby is accommodated and staying together to know each other.
Risk management seminar will be held at the same time.

Team Pink panther

Rock Rugby

Team Pink Panther with Senor Sergeant(Gunso san)

Members from university of the Ryukyu

Zamami members with Occhi san

7th All Japan Rock Rugby Competition at Tokashi Island

Team Pink Panther

Zamami members at Tokashiki Island

Rock Rugby is
 so exciting!!!

Everyone is preparing
 with skill up!

Looking forward to meeting at all Japan competition in November.

Life saving

Life saving

Lifesaving is social activity of saving life, for prevention of accidents at waterside.

It seems difficult if say as above, lifesaving is covering activities such as supervising at seaside or swimming pools, rescue activities and all kinds of related activities.

Mmmm, still difficult?

In another word, To save life from accident of waterside, do best prevention of accident and Rescue.

Not only guarding at waterside,but also holding safety classes,

Cardio-pulmonary resuscitation, clean up at coast for enjoying waterside.

Guarding and leadership rescue, competitions for improving technical skills for lifesaving are all covered.

Japan Lifesaving Assocation(JLA) is aiming Zero accident at water side.

Necessary to get special knowledge and skills for guarding and lifesaving at seaside and swimming pools.

License which have been approved by JLA through receiving qualifications workshops.

Life saving

300,000 per year! Every 2 minutes! What is this number ?

It is the number of losing lives all over the world at waterside!

But, most of cases are caused by careless miss, or inattention, like not warming up before swimming, swimming after drinking.

Of course,some cases due to nature disasters,but some of them can be prevented by our own mind.

So to prevent sad accident,wish to get knowledge and technical skills of lifesaving.

Activities conducted by JLA are as follows.

One is sport

Physical fitness and technical skills are essential to save life in case accident occurs.

In fact, It is very dangerous to have big waves and strong tides.

To save drowning man,Physical fitness is essential, so we are practicing day by day and improving own technique.

Occhi san(Mr.Otsuji) leader of our saving team keeps telling us to do training.

Life saving competition are holding for competing our own achievement and improving our own skills at various places in the world.

Second is Education.

Life saving include our own lives and family's lives, too.

So I myself do not cause waterside accident. My own life protect by myself.

Holding Safety classes are best solution for preventing accident.

JLA is holding various types of safety classes for youth and adults as mentioned before.

And Welfare and Environment

With developing activities using the knowledge and skills of life saving.

Wish to have correct knowledge to enjoy bathing, fishing, Swimming at swimming pool, playing at waterfront.

The certification of Japan Lifesaving Association are Cardio-pulmonary resuscitation, water lifesaving, surf lifesaving and IRB(Emergency boat) at the level of beginner to advance, instructor.

Cabinet Office NPO Japan Lifesaving Association
http://www.jla.gr.jp/

JLA is the representative institutions in Japan as International Life Saving Federation (ILS) a national organization on life saving certified to a specific NPO In Japan.

Kadena Health Promotion Centre

Occhi san worked there and looking for part time workers who are young swimmers and shouted to swimming club members of university of the Ryukyu.
That was a opportunity to have such a close communications each other.

Thanks for meeting everyone

Starbucks at Chatan

I am not good at coffee, so my favorite is sweat drink.

Held a speical cinema event of Water Rock Rugby at Chatan Starbucks with special permission from them.
It was so dynamic since big size of screen there.

We normally drop and eat Curry rice, Okinawa Soba after our activities.
It is so nice!!!
Yushi Dofu Soba is my recommendation at Hamaya.

Yushi Dofu Soba

Our home Coast at Chatan town.
(Miyagi Coast)

Triathlon at Miyako Island
Joined as support members with Occhi san, It is tremendous !!
Over 1500 Participants are swimming.

Occhisan lent me it when I lost my clock, It was with me since then, even I said when I buy new one, return to you,,,,
But,It is always with me when I go to the sea, even from now on,,,,

I learnt "body surfing" there,
               without board.
It is possible only when big waves are there!
                        So exciting.

Chatan Miyagi Coast

One of TV station came to have a interview for Water Rock Rugby on their TV program called 'Osaka Honwaka TV'.

At that time I had a chance to see it and got a lecture of lifesaver with my friend Haruki.
I have got basic lifesaver's license with Haruki and Rika half year later.
It seems 10 years absences after Occhi-san has got it as University student in Okinawa.
I have got advances license, too.

When the opening ceremony of Okinawa Prefecture branch of Japan Lifesaving Association,
Three of us, Haruki, Rika and I who have got the license have been introduced there.

Life saving

Lecture by Otono san

Passing from Toyoda san

Has got Lifesaving License !!

Thank you

Advance course at Gino-wan
Tropical Beach(Practice)
Mari-rin Ginowan (Lecture)
Nov.2010

Practical activities so cold,,,,,

Opening Ceremony of Okinawa Branch of JLA

受検番号：006
No 006

修 了 証
Certification

 殿

for Mr.Dai Morishita

あなたは、日本ライフセービング協会認定のアドバンス・サーフ・ライフセーバー講習会において、定められた全てのプログラムを修了したことをここに証します。

You have completed all program of advanced surf lifesaving course cerified by JLA.

平成 **22**年 **11**月 **15**日
15th Nov 2010

内閣府特定非営利活動法人　日本ライフセービング協会

理事長　小峯　力
指導員　豊田　勝義

Japan Lifesaving Association
President Riki Komine
Instructor Katsuyoshi Toyoda

Life saving

Oh I am on the Poster of Lifesaving Club without knowing it.

It seems that my photo is better than others...

Role of Lifeguard is to prevent accident not rescue.
So In case any emergency accident, it should be on our fault since cannot find any risk in advance.

Lifesaving In Zamami

Lifesaving members at University of the Ryukyu have got chances to work as lifeguard at Zamami Island arranged by Occhi san.

I am introducing Zamami Island.

Locating about 40 km from Naha City.

Zamami Island is centre of Zamami Village located west side of Tokashiki Village.

Zamami Village is islands village which consists from Zamami, Aka, and Geruma which are all inhabited islands, and also Yakabi, Kuba, Amuro and others uninhabited islands.

Zamami Island are one of main island of Kerama Islands same as Tokashiki Island.

It is good to come Zamami Island taking ferry from Tomarin in Okinawa Island.

The contrast Blue of Sea and Black on Rock is magnificent.

Most of Zamami Island is covered by Forest. Kerama Deer come across to village in night.

Zamami Island is rather popular since population and number of tourist are not so small even isolated island.

Most of tourist are divers and whale watcher in winter season.

Life saving

In addition there are 5 Observatories so you can enjoy island scenery.

The sea in Zamami island has been ranking 2-star Michelin Green Guide Japan in 2009.

As for us lifeguard members are staying Communal living at cottage. We normally do self-catering,and most of material are getting by ourselves at the sea.

We cook big Octpus,Okoze which we get by ourselves,and learn how to cook from Occhisan
Enjoy cooking & eating supported by people in the island.
Sometimes enjoying with tourists.

In addition,We really love to take bath together with guys.
It seems like school trip.
It is ceremony of trust each other
We cannot stop it even Occhisan try to stop it. Wow,,

With Mika

Marilyn in Zamami Island

Siro in Aka Island

As you may know the movie titled "Want to meet my Marilyn", Siro in Aka Island and Marilyn in Zamami, they are falling love each other.

Mika came to Zamami by herhself,so next day,I took a day off and took her to Aka Island.
It seems Marilyn & Siro.
Far-love has been started

Stars at Zamami is marvelous even we can see beautiful stars in Okinawa Island.

If I could tell names of stars to girlfriend, it would be so nice,,,

With Bobby Oregon when he came as private holiday

with Rescue members

Kerama Deer which are Natural monument, it is seldom to see them, but sometimes, we can see them so often.

Job of life guards sometimes give information like dangerous area around the island to enjoy beaches at the Zamami Island in addition with rescue and supervising at the beach.
Of course people from foreign countries, Even I can guess they are where coming from by hearing their accents.
I can meet many people coming from all over the world here.
It is so exciting !

It is Best thing doing lifeguard!

Lifeguard Diary of Zamami

20th Sep (2009) Spring tide Day2 Winds from North east Wave 3-5m
Furuzamami Beach Otsuji-san Teppei, Hiroshi, and Dai
Ama Beach Bob-san Kosetsu, Haruki

High 7:55 227 cm Low 13:57

	Beach	Sea	Total	Tide	Wave	Wind
9:00	10	5	15	L->R	0-0.5	North
10:00	35	25	60	as above		
11:00	130	80	210	as above		
12:00	100	50	150	as above		
13:00	125	100	225	as above		
14:00	125	110	235	as above		
15:00	95	100	195	as above		
16:00	80	80	160	as above		
17:00	25	10	35	as above		

8:40 Rescue training

<FA> 8
9:00 M 30 Okinawa Kuchin
9:05 F 22 Fukuoka Left Hand
12:30 M 40 Taman Rock area Finger
12:45 F 30 Saitama Right hand
14:30 M 40 Taman Left hand
13:30 M 30
15:50 M 30 Right cut

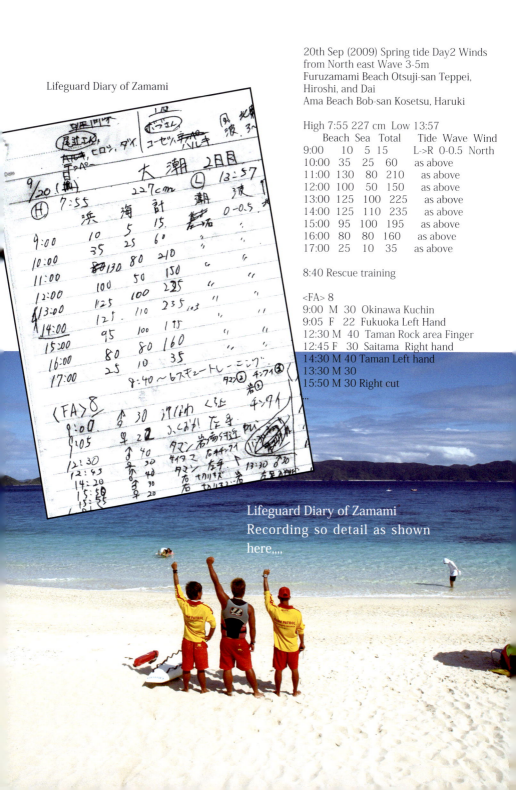

Lifeguard Diary of Zamami
Recording so detail as shown here,,,,

I love the sea very much, but I have no chance to win Occhi-san's love for the sea.

Keys of enjoying a day as good as I can

Do what to do

- Do my job
- Make Schedule
- Get up early
- Talk with my sweet girlfriend
- Do exercise
- something like taking protein
- Be positive

Diver

Octopus in cottage

The sunset in Zamami

Sea turtle's baby

Stopped the ferry at Zamami

At Zamami, it was arranged to see off our friends who have worked there by lifeguard members as surprise.

At that time I was on the ferry to catch up to work as lifeguard.

Originally the plan was that after departure, try to see off by small boat. I was also expected to be the members of seeing off after quickly getting off the ferry.

Since nobody could find me at the quay, everybody thought that Dai should be the next ferry.

Then the ferry has been departed,but it did not move any more just staying at the port,,,

What happened? Lifeguard members wondered why the ferry stopped in the middle of port, after a while, the ferry started and could see me on small boat!

The reason why, I was on the small boat, I was just waked up by hearing whistling for departure of the ferry, so I was late to get off the ferry,,,!!

Even I asked the captain to return to the quary, it was refused, so I said, I am trying to jumping into the sea. It is so dangerous, it should not be, And finally the small boat helped me to ride there

This is the unprecedented story stopping the ferry at At Zamami

(It was first time at Zamami, I was strictly warned by the authorities)

Life saving

Stung by a Jellyfish

On my way to the beach for lifeguard, I jumped into the sea since Occhi-san advised here is so beautiful, but Just after jumped into the sea, I have got a keen pain, and got out immediately.

Even Occhi-san dived into the sea, jellyfish has not been found.

Oh dear, Occhi-san, I have pain on my back!!

It must be hub jellyfish!

Occhi-san said, There is no hub jellyfish in Kerama Islands, it may be Andon Jellyfish.

Anyway it has poison, I was feeling so sad on that day

People in Kerama village said it may be hub jellyfish by looking at my skin bite by jellyfish.

It was also a just joke, no way,

I put dry ice which gotten from the shop onto the point bitten by jellyfish for keeping cold.

After pain gone, I found my skin became frostbite.

Double punches,

It was terrible day, everyone laughed me even I had big pain,,

Hub Jellyfish habitat in only Okinawa prefecture In Japan, especially in summer season,it will be appearing around the sea in Okinawa
It has strong poison and quite dangerous in case small children bitten.
If bitten by hub jellyfish,put vinegar on the skin directly.
Andon Jellyfish live from Hokkaido to Okinawa, small size jellyfish. In case bitten by them
Has pain with numb.

Both jellyfish is dangerous organisms in the sea. we can enjoy the sea with basic knowledge and first aid for those living things.

Chromis viridis(deba suzume dai) in the Zamami's sea

Archeology

It is so difficult, struggling and felt not good for me, but,

It might be affected by my parents who took me various places at many occasion.

drawing In Ihara First shelter

Archeology

People who study 『Archeology』

History is mainly based on written material.
Archeology is mainly based on real object.
Such as tools which someone made, place people lived, material culture which made by human being.
For person who study archeology, normally they like object,,,
Children who like to collect are good for studying archeology.
In fact there are many of them those who study archeology had been collectors.
Normally we call such person Ko-ko boy(archeology boy)
Collecting marble, figures, something, remember dorama's story A to Z, can tell all series of Hero stories, history mania, as such, if you may have something to enthusiasm, you are entitled to be called monozuki(little strange person), and can stand in front of archeology.
In my Seminal, some of my friends say
cannot throw away anything which are keeping since their nursery days, Habit to pick something up on the road like bolt.
Would like to work at museum as work experience at primary school.

Welcome party for newcomers at the seminal 《MAC competition》

MAC competition is arranged at welcome party for newcomers of our seminal to compete how many hamburger can be eaten, because newcomers are under 20 years old should be no alcohol.

It is first time to see so many hamburgers at once.

As for me, ate 7 or 8 hamburgers,,

Steady work of archeology

Sometimes, we have chance to meet news like
Great Discovery of century Excavated something at XXX Remains
But, there are unbelievable tough job until this great discovery.
No promise even you dig, you may not excavate anything,,
I will show you how tough archeology is.
Here I will show a really part of tough job,
But I should say this is just introduction
how to study archeology at university,
since we are just standing at the corner
of archeology.

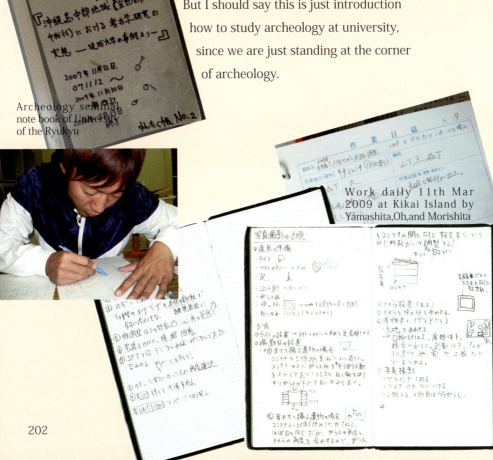

Archeology seminar note book of University of the Ryukyu

Work daily 11th Mar 2009 at Kikai Island by Yamashita, Oh, and Morishita

Tool for measuring relic

Like this you can attach this tool to relic

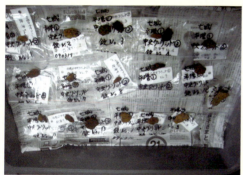

Relics from Nana-Jyo remains at Kikai Island of Kagojima prefecture

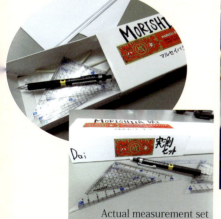

Actual measurement set

My own seven tools boxing in my favorite sweat

Recording remain's name, excavated point, excavated date on the side of small relic. One by one
It is very hard work to record with small character one by one, after this work, will store with soring out.

Maritime Archaeology

「What is Archeology in the sea?」

Archeology with investigation and researching in the sea.

Ruins sank to the seabed by crustal movement, environmental changes, and most cases are sunken ship to be targets.

We can find those days' lives and technologies specifically, and marine traffic, transportation, realities of trades from sunken ships.

On the other hand, recently scuba became popular and easier to act in the water by improving technology, destroying remains' risk becoming higher.

Due to this circumstances, protection of submarine's cultural property is a issue on survey of sunken ships.

Treatment for remaining in the sea are some different among countries.

For example,

Western Europe…ownership will remain on original owner even after several hundred years.

China, the Philippines, others… Ownership wll be shifted to the country where sunken and left for certain years.

Maritime Archaeology

While the direction of cultural property protection advance in the world, there are some cases which cultural properties withdrawn from the sea are in auctions, and dissipation.

In this circumstance, Salvaged wrecked with supported by the government in 1978 as early stage at Shin-an in Korea.

In this thesis, I would like to study the importance of maritime archeology, or possibility.

Thesis exercise December 2010 Prologue

The monument of Genko(Attack by Gen) at Takashima Nagasaki Prefecture
Takashima is famous for the island where attacked by Gen so called GEN Ko.
There are many remains
Especially at the Koan no Eki(1281),Gen's many ships mooring in Takashima bay have been sunken by the storm.
So Takashima bay are famous for remains which tell the history of Gen-Ko attack in 1281

The monument of Gen Ko Attack iat Takashima

Archeology in the sea

Just after joining the university, what I like is just Sea. That is all!
I have been really enjoying my college life getting many friends playing at the sea, doing marine sports.
As for Geography Anthropology which I choose in the University,
I have searched the seminal which can combine with the sea, then
I found maritime archeology which archeology in the sea.
I like history, so that I tried to visit Professor Ikeda.
He advised there is no chance to study maritime archeology in the sea immediately for those who cannot study archeology on the land.

He lead me to learn archeology on the land first, because if you study maritime archeology you should breathe, talk each other and see in the sea same as on the land.

Map of Takashima island
It seems a lot of remains which of sunken shipped at the time of Genko over 700 years ago around Takashima Island's bottom of the sea in Matsuura City Nagasaki Prefecture Japan.
Professor Ikeda studies wreck in Takashima Island.

Maritime Archaeology

Boring survey at Takashima Island remains August 2009

Professor Ikeda took me to survey at Takashima on my 2nd and 3rd grade after studying archeology on the land as he advised.

But at first time, I was just watching how to prepare the survey.

How to proceed survey in the sea, I know that basic procedure on the land, so even on the land digging relic, a lot of soils, dust, it is also tough.

So you can imagine if in the sea what happens,,

When dig in the sea, it become muddy, so cannot see anything at all.

Only the person get used to it,can do work,

Even Professional Diver may lose direction in the sea!

There are Indication board at survey area for taking over of diver,

Communicate progress of survey by showing which direction diver

Underwater position sonic exploration equipment (transmission & Reception)

Equipment of Video and Audio Receiver Underwater

is facing and location of divers.

I found that I cannot do anything at all since I do not know which direction I am facing even right or left,,

So Professor Ikeda kindly gave me a chance to show all works to understand and do myself.

Now I am just starting to understand what is going on by his guidance.

After this training, I had got a chance to stay in Australia by suspended university for one year.

As for diving I have got skill to survive in the sea, so next stage is that to accumulate experience what to be done in the sea as archaeologist.

I am still not that stage yet. Working in the sea has three stages,

Camera and Light underwater photography(Video)

Situation of attaching underwater position sonic exploration equipment on Hull

Maritime Archaeology

Shooting Underwater photography(Video)

Underwater position sonic exploration equipment(Transporter)

first one is to get experience, second is to gain knowledge, and third is to gain technology.

I am just getting experience just on the surface.

When I joined with the survey for my first time, I had a chance to see what were there.

At the first boring survey, but, I could not do excavation work yet.

When I dived as my first time, I help to put the bar setting survey area.

I checked the distance one by one after followed by Professor putting the bar every one meter.

I really thought that I would like to study Ko-Ko(maritime archeology) ! by getting real experience.

Survey in the Kanzaki port of Takashima Island

Underwater Photography(geographical features)

Oct 2009 Takashima underwater ruins prospecting survey

1.Departure to plots 2.Fixing work of ship 3.Underwater mud transfer device 4.Monitoring Underwater position sc exploration equipment 5.Buoy to the plots 6.Preparation of diving equipment 7.Hose of Underwater mud transfer device sucked up relics protection device 8.Excavated material with nail holes(wooden) 9.Description board of plots 10.Excava material(wood) 11.Excavated material(wood) 12.Storage of excavated materials on the board 13.Description board of sur status(for taking over of diving) 14.Resin impregnation equipment to the wood at Takashima Archaeological Centre

Maritime Archaeology

出 張 依 頼 書

平成 21 年 9 月 26 日

森 下 大 殿

国立大学法人琉球大学
教授 池田栄史

科学研究費補助金による研究の遂行のため、貴殿に下記の出張をお願い申し上げます。

記

1、出 張 者　　森下 大

2、用　　務　　鷹島海底遺跡潜水調査の補助

3、用 務 地　　長崎県松浦市

4、用 務 先　　松浦市教育委員会および同市立鷹島埋蔵文化財センター
　　　　　　　　鷹島海底遺跡周辺海域

5、出 張 日 程　平成 21 年 10 月 1 日 ～ 平成 21 年 10 月 6 日

6、費用の負担
　　　平成 21 年度科学研究費基盤研究（S）
　　　研究課題名　長崎県北松浦郡鷹島周辺海底に眠る元寇関連遺跡・遺物の把握と解明
　　　課題番号　18102004
　　　研究代表者　琉球大学・法文学部・教授・池田栄史

Request of Business Trip

26th September 2009

Attention to Mr.Dai Morishita　　　National University Corporation
　　　　　　　　　　　　　　　　　University of the Ryukyus
　　　　　　　　　　　　　　　　　Professor Eishi Ikeda

Request of Business Trip for the execution of the study by Grant-in-Aid for Scientific Research.

Note

1. Name　　Dai Morishita
2. Role　　Assistant works of Takashima underwater ruins diving survey
3. Place　　Matsuura City Nagasaki Prefecture
4. Destination Matsuura City Board of Education and Takashima reserves Cultural Centre
   Takashima underwater ruins surrounding area
5. Schedule　1st October 2009 --- 6th October 2009
6. The burden of cost　rant-in-Aid for Scientific Research on 2009 (S)
   Title of project
   Understanding and clarification of Gen Ko Attak related ruins, relics sleeping
   Takashima Island Kita Matsuura County Nagasaki Prefecture
   Project Number 18102004
   Project leader　Professor Eishi Ikeda
   Faculty of Law and Literature University of the Ryukyus

213

Minimum factors for studying maritime Archaeology

There are suitable or unsuitable in the sea to study maritime archeology. It is impossible for the person who cannot swim, either dive.

Especially survey in the sea, it may happen that cannot do things which normally can do on the land if you are not confident with swimming ,no chance to do anything.

The person who is good at settling down in the sea,can stay quietly even something may happen during diving.

Even expert of archeology, who is not good at the sea, it is very hard to do something in the sea.

From this point,I am sure that I am suitable for maritime Archeology. Professor Ikeda thought so and took me the survey.

Even there are many students in the seminal, but the Professor did not take any student at all.

Although he tried some students to take, but no one wished to go.

Yes, Underwater is very tough.

Joined excavation survey in Takashima Island

Archeology is 『Usho』 of the Ukai

Usho is leader of Ukai which is one of the traditional fishing by using Cormorant in Japan.

Person who is diving into the sea is U(U:Cormorant) in Ukai

U is taking fishes in the water, but Usho shows the direction to take fishes.

U is taking fishes under Usho's control.

Now I am going to dive based on direction,so I can be U.

I am not at the stage which can see all activities of survey.

If I am like now, I may be staying to continue to dive.

I have to study archeology more.

To become Usho, I have to gain archeology knowledge and accumulate more experiences in the sea.

So I am learning now.

What can I do in the maritime Archeology?

I am confident with diving, but not enough competence for purpose, activities on the survey.

I am a U not Usho yet.

I have to study more to be Usho. Archeology for recognizing purposes and methodology, Maritime Archeology.

To do so, What I should do, I have to read books more.

Just I have started to study to get basic knowledge of surveys in the world, and read literature for basic archeology.

Reading books of history is current target for me. It seems recognized what I need.

Maritime Archeology is not perfectly established yet, Even I can be a pioneer !

Archeology in the sea is under going to be established.

So I study it, I can have a chance in this world.

That means I can be a pioneer who can open by own power on the maritime Archeology.

Searching ships of Gen Ko Attack coming from Mongolia is Professor Ikeda's Theme.

In fact, Last year, Professor Ikeda found the remains of Gen ko ships unfortunately I was away to Australia.

He keeps his survey so that if I learn under Professor Ikeda, it is ready to get good experiences.

I am really lucky, becauce there is quite seldom where has seminal can learn maritime Archeology in Japan.

To become a maritime archaeologist

To become a maritime archaeologist,
At first love the sea.
To be interested in studying something with the sea.
To get wider view with the sea like studying geology of the seabed, Organisms in the sea.
Something like this merging with study .
If only love the sea is just hobby, but if I can study the sea,it may make me stronger, so called Oni ni kanabo meaning that Strong man with weapon
There are many students who like archeology, but not so many who also like the sea.
To tell the truth,Professor Goto,another professor in the seminal does not like the sea,,
So if takes him to the sea,he may be getting away immediately.
Professor Ikeda is a diver and archeologist. If I say Diving in Japanese Moguri which means unofficial archeologist!
It is quite interesting there are something related with human in the sea.

What can I do with learning Archeology in the future?

Archeology is attractive since once being interested in Archeology, hard to quit from it.

Survey normally need hard physical work,then physics and spirit should be merging into one.

So I can feel happiness and accomplishment extraordinary which cannot be gotten from other studies.

Once you get this feeling, you cannot forget it and occur symptoms of poisoning.

It is very tough, very hot and even very dirty, without these difficulties, I cannot get real accomplishment, so I will continue.

Someone in the seminal said that, I am almost giving up, but keeping on just about.

One more important thing,

Archeology cannot be done by oneself. It only can be done by all.

We can overcome tough issues by corporation among all.

And pleasure also become bigger since done by all.

Of course,some of part must be done by oneself,like writing thesis,and thinking but Survey must be done by all.

Covering each other makes strong team work.

Continue to study Archeology is slightly higher than other courses, since administrative works are demanding.

Great Discovery 《Found Remains of Ships at Gen ko Attack!!》

Professor Ikeda's press release on 24th Oct 2011!!

Professor Ikeda had ruins investigation to Takashima Island in Nagasaki prefecture 2011 again.

He called me up to go to survey, with him but I could not make it. Finally he found it!

There are places where I was taken by him two years ago.and dived into the sea and taught by Professor what should we do, supported boring survey.

Even last year he did survey on the same place.

Survey of maritime archaeology is really tough work, since in the sea.

Working with experienced divers who fully understand the survey,searching remains hampered by seawater, soils.

The year before last year, Professor made marks on the spot, and prepared .

Finally has found sunken ship of Gen ko Attack in the sea!!

At least more than 20 meters span's big size of Ship.

As first time it has been found with recognizing shape of the

Maritime Archaeology

bottom.
It is really Brilliant achievement!
It seems that about half of hull was appeared by this survey.
Professor Ikeda talked on the press media that would like to show all part of ships by finding Information of Bow and Stern.

Congratulations Professor Ikeda!!

It is tremendous! TV programs showed his press release covering all Japan wide, and on the newpapers' articles are so wide.
Sensei hom-ma sugoiwa!! (Great! Professor Ikeda)
If I were joined the survey, I could be a small part of TV screen at press release.
Where is Dai? Many of divers who know me asked as such,,Oh dear.

Asashi Newspaper
24th Oct 2011
Take off large navy veil

March 2012 the ruins are defined as National historical landmark at first time as underwater ruins

Mainichi Newspaper 24th Oct 2011
Even 730 years ago the legendary elucidation

What I would like to talk to Professor Ikeda

● It is true that I would like to work at JICA(Japan International Cooperation Agency) or Tokyo Fire Department,
I know that you may advise me it is impossible for you,,
But I would like to take examination seriously.

● After graduate school
 I cannot make my own image when I am working.
 I would like to know more

● Both getting Job and going to the graduate school are very attractive,
So that I would like to keep putting my antenna to catch various information.

● I am very pleased to be recommended to go to the graduate school so much, I also try to do it.

● Thank you so much Professor Ikeda

With Professor Ikeda(left) and Professor Goto(Right)

25th Nov 2010 Get to work Note

Going to Australia suspended School life!!

It seems so attractive.

Kick off to get something new for me, like I have got in Okinawa.
Coming one year, it will be so important.
Became interested in English
Recognize how tough to get money to survive.

Journey moving!

   Anyway moving !!

Anyway People !!

   Meet people and farewell

10/4/2010

Farewell messages from Rock Rugby friends,,

Birthday messages from university friends

Messages from Life servers in 2009

If I don't decide my target yet,
do not have to make any plan.

So I will live now slowly and steadily.

Australia Note

Don't neglect
Risk Management!!

- Keep my luggage separately
- Keep information memo(like Passport number)
- Be flexible for unexpected matters

To Do List 3/7
- ☐ Exchange
- ☐ Purchase bay pack (40-60l) Cheeper
- ☐   Sleep bag   → Not necessary to rush
- ☐ Decide the plan after School
- ☐ Search about FARM
    - ← Peeler Farm is only two one is Bleom other is Kains
        Also at Darwin,too

April 5   Mon 6:45
Sydney → Adelaide $ $89
→Shall I get a ticket soon after getting confirmation with David！！

I must practice first before I go (school)
Otherwise no meaning

☆ Make Vocabulary Note of Harry Potter !

To Adelaide
By Air $ 99 Morning
By Bus $142 Wed or Sun 2:55pm Next Day's 6:40 Arrive
Depends on Surfboard

21/3
13:00 mail to Araki,Ikemachi regarding with Jillian ,David,and Kimura
Padiss Market Bag* Cloters
　→ Kinokuniya　→ Complete draft of Insurance → talk with Tohikyo
Minneapolis Cres 2/65 2035
Searching Farm
・Take Surfboard or
・Not take train?

Schedule
Sydney Central 4/5 19:00-
Melbourne　7:00
Melbourne southern Cross Station
Spencer St. 8:40 am 7:10
Adelaide 17:45 pm Arrival

Rough Plan

4 ------------------------ 9

　Australia---------

9 Zamami how can I prepare for getting job !

10 preparation for getting job,or

↓

5 months later, I will be Okinawa

From tomorrow I will work,,

To be honest,now(16th April,2010) I am not interested in maritime

Archeology ,,,

It may become interesting once starting,,,

I will expect so,and better concentrate on things until September

Maritime Archeology

I will watch what I am aiming.

April May June July Aug

Only 5 month left!!

3 month at Farm   → 2 month worst case in September !!

　　I am very glad to be here in Australia,
　　Since I can think like that. I would like to try more.

Time goes first

    Faster than expecting

Many of things

    I do not know the right answer

Anyway, Thanks and Pleasure!

21/4/2010 18:10 In Living room HOT

Today we don't have work .actually. we don't have work 4days from today.
I'm in Renmark working for Amaloo orange farm.
I have worked 4 times already and I can get 150backs per day. Not too bad.

But, there is a problem.
The problem is holiday.
So boring, everybody become like rubbish.

What I did today is just hong out town, went to library, supermarket,,,,
As for another guys, there were just sleeping all day.

Fujiya Japanese Restaurant in Sydney   Fujiya's Entrance

Going to Australia suspended School life!!

Especially, the German guy who is staying with me doesn't have any job,
so everyday he is like rubbish.

He really makes me annoy, Ok I'm gonna read Harry potter !!
see you !

I'm ganna work in Amaloo from tomorrow again. I'm thinking,,

I'd like a word Lupin

「You have nothing to feel ashamed of.
What's that supposed to be?」

(From Harry Potter)

> Morishita Dai's English short course
> I'm parched.　→　I'm so hungry.

Will

Japan E - E

　(learn experience as experience)

Overseas E – K

　(learn experience as knowledge)

Both are important

Because I have my own will

for studying maritime Archeology,

Going to the graduate school means

　　　　I will follow the Professor.

Going to Australia suspended School life!!

Well that sounds helpful.

I am thinking about continue to study archaeology in master's degree.
I wanna know or not it is really worth stud for me.

Studying Archaeology is well worth studying in master degree's or not.
I think it's very important to meet people who study Maritime archaeology for me.
I want to know what sort of people study Maritime archaeology.
I am in Australia.

He introduces what he is studying and people who work with him.
But I should study more about archaeology.
I have studied already just for 1 year.

After going back to Japan,
I'm going to study more and think I should study more
Maritime Archaeology or not.

I think I have a lot of choices I would like to meet a lot of various people and feel something.

My Professor Mr.Ikeda he has a lot of major likes a old battle field cannon.

I am pleased to meet you.

Thanks a lot.

Surfing
Better get surf board in Australia and take it back to Okinawa or not,,,
  I will ask Byron ,,,one idea that do surfing,,,
  And check how much to take it back to Okinawa
  Whether long or short,,,

Rock(Rugby)
I really wish to meet all with Rock Rugby.
Try to make my breathe longer
Need to do muscle training
Do not want to be embarrassed

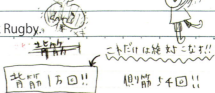

Muscles of the back 10,000time!!
Should practice at least!!
Lateral muscle 54 times!!

Swimming
  Will change to fee style,,
  Wish to swim so much

Free Style
Anyway muscle strength,endurance
Swim long distance
Want to swim！！！

Study
  Earnestness do steadily

10／5／2010

Just less than one month has gone after coming to Renmark,
I do not know how will be with Emily.
I will work tomorrow!!

13／6／2010

Oh
I have a choice,
whether continue to stay in Australia for 2 years continuously or back to Okinawa.
Once I will be back to Okinawa,,
nnnn,, Yes I will stay here ,,! Smiling,,

My writing became not tidy.
Australia is beautiful.

7.31 LastBus
Cannot find my i-Pod!!
Regrettable!
Buy i-Pod or Touch

English is so difficult not as like crying yet,

 I will study hard targeting TOEIC examination at the end of November.
 I will try to score 800 seriously!!
 Maybe 500 now,,,

Chant — Song — Sing
Better buy word note!!

Note
The World isn't split into good people and death eaters inspect.
Get a grip on yourself
Nudge = touch Push

"Look on the bright sight"

Morishita Dai's English short course
I'll bet.　→　I thought so!.

Going to Australia suspended School life!!

I will go to the library to get information more around at Noosa on 15th and stay at Fraser Island two nights,
then after going down to Sunshine Coast.

Finally will back to Brisbane on 26th, or try to go somewhere else,,
Or Nudist WWOOF World Wide Opportunities on Organic Farms,
Anyway I will move as I like at that time.
I will continue to read Harry Potter and should be ready for reading 7th Vol after backing to Japan immediately.

To do at Sydney
- Buy a surf board if I will decide to buy
- Go to Manly Beach
- Pray Opera house officially at last
- Go to Thai restaurant
    (Famous but do not remember the name)
- Do not be late for the flight

Muscle training and Uhama
- Try training abdominal muscles, back muscles, push-ups until rising up
- Bicycle and Running
- Breath-hold intention to breath
- Review of Rope work   Aim Gun dam !!

2.8.10

The day before yesterday, I lost my i-Pod

I did it !

New one is so good something like dictionary instead of i-Pod!

Today I will take 14:00 bus to go to 2nd WWOOF !!

Coorey

I wish it is good place !

Now I'm at Burger shop in south bank.

Emily thanks for everything

2.8.10 ～ 13.8.10

11Days → 80+11= 91Days Enough

Arriving at Brisbane

Because I lost my i-Pod, use this for keeping dairy, changing dailylife is something good.

Harry Potter

Read 5th volume by mid Aug, 6th in September,

and 7th in Japanese

Going to Australia suspended School life!!

Cuisine teaching from Mrs.K.Irie

Mrs.Kiyoko Irie is my parents' friends in UK when my family was in Cardiff.

Especially she took care of me a lot when I was just born.

She is so kind since like changing my nappy when I was a new baby born.

I was trying to see her because she is living in Australia now.

I have stayed at her house for a few days,and learned cooking for my girlfriend in Australia.

It was so successful and could have good time with her,,,,

Menu learned from Mrs.K.Irie

1,Carrot Salad
   I have got a recipes from her, tried to all taste of mayonnaise, Ketchup, and Mustard.

2,Ox tongue
   Challenge to make it my own favorite, cooked it by myself from preparation.
   Two types of cooking
   ① Take Ox tongue's skin by raw   ② Take Ox tongue's skin after boiling
   I preferred first one

Morishita Dai's English short course
Are you kidding? → Are you sure???.

My family came to see me in Australia!!

6th Aug 2010 What to do at library

Send mail to WWOOF at PPP to ask in detail.

Before this, ask whether can stay here until 13th

Check anyplace to be dropped between Fraser and PPP.

Sydney   27th Oct 2009 til 2nd April 2010
Melbourne 3rd April -- 10th April
Adelaide   12th April – 16th April
Renmark   16th April -- 27th June
Brisbane   28th June – 6th July
Cairns   7th July – 13th July
Yalbooo   14th July – 31st July
Brisbane
Cooney
PPP
Ailie
Brisbane

19th Aug 2010(tomorrow)
I am leaving WWOOF at Nudist here,
Host family seems so strange, all the time,
Orgeing! Enough!
So noisy! If only Mike not so but,,
My leisure time is only reading Harry Potter,,
I'm free, either no schedule at all,
Perhaps, on Thur and Fri will be at Ailsede
And on Sat, Sun, Mon, sailing or islands tour,
then on Tue back to Brisbane!

19th Aug 2010
What I should not forget,,,
get a present for Dad.

Cannot believe only less than twenty days until back to Japan,,
Anyway, how much I can read 7th Vol Harry Potter!
Will finish 6th a.s.a.p.
Use 500 Dollars for surfboard from Tax refund.

All my family joined at Sydney   So good,,,

Ton-Katsu(Pork cutlet), Ochazuke,Karaage(fried chiken), Tamago gohan(egg rice), Tendon and Sushi

Now I really want to eat Pork cutlet ,Ochazuke,fried chiken, egg rice,Tendon and Sushi

And, Mackerel, Salted ox Tongue also want to eat, but Ton-Katsu is best!

U,,,,

Once going back to Japan,Shall we go eating, my friends,,,

For these two weeks, I have been working with family who is vegetarian.
So What I have eaten is only vegetable and fruit, So Good digestion

At least 3 times a day of toilet, so powerful isn't it
Better eat vegetable more especially for the person are constipation

Going to Australia suspended School life!!

How much ate bananas,,
took vegetable at the garden for lunch,,

Then now I just arrived back to Brisbane by flight.

From the day after tomorrow I will learn cooking by Papua New Guinea's lady!
How good!

After back to Okinawa,,Give me a refrigerator, rice cooker, and washing machine,,
Really need ,,or
Shall we live together someone!

By the way, when I visited Cairns
Went to World heritage the Great barrier Leaf, but Okinawa's sea is more beautiful

Shark there, that's all!

As for me,
I became to be able to eat Tomato

How important after back

to Japan!!

listen English all the time and read!

More things to want to do,

More things to have to do,

will enjoy both with good balance!

10/8/2010

My lunch is only 1$ bread for last one week due to lack of money,.
Met Yasu and Taiki they are in Australia as I am there.
Many of my friends in Australia like Osa,. and Mika also came to see me ♡

Going to Australia suspended School life!!

Thinking

As for thinking there are four theme such as Present, Past, Future and Delusion

Definitely main for us is present not past either future ,delusion.
Future and present seems same ,but should be thinking mainly with present.
When you are concentrating on one thing, such as club activities, study, reading book, work so on,
Balance of these elements is balance of a day.
Thinking can be reserved until going to bed!
Not thinking too much makes me more interesting, I am thinking like this now.

Writing like this,it is already not matching what I said just now, (Hahaha)
Life becomes more interesting by having more experience and meeting many people.
There are more people than I thought in the world, change common sense all the time.

JAPAN

Definitely there is no way to end with this one year to live in any foreign country in my life.
Absolutely I will have time to wish to go abroad again, but I would like to know how is Japan now.

In fact, I think Japan is good,
but not so exciting if I would be in Japan all the time.

My presence in the world is less than a dot,but from my point of view, this is all.
So that it is better to change the world by changing my point of view as I can satisfy!

Whenever I want to write something, what is good for me to write?
What I want to eat what I want to express my feeling.
To do list. Experience is good, but I am scarring budist.

Anxienty for overseas

There is anxiety for going to overseas.
I had chance to get support from the person of language school when I am going to work holiday.
Mr.Tamura supervise APLac.

There are many articles seniors essays ,messages directly at APLac.
I also made some sentences over there.

It was upload with introduction of me on the APLac site/
I will show you on next page,I am so shy!

> Morishita Dai's English short course
> I knew it.   →   as I thought

This is the one from Osaka for working holiday interrupted his University life in Okinawa, he is a nice guy.

His experiences are really nice with full his native Osaka dialect.

He said that I am not good at writing and tried to write but threw away 2 pieces of paper,

But once completed it, his essay is impacting and interesting with his real voices like he is talking with his Osaka dialect directly.

It is very easy to understand, Aura is so huge than the contents.

So please take his words like as sunbathing.

Just reading sentences may give you impression like an active wild guy, but he is rather quiet and shy.

He did not want to show his video in public since he is shy, I guess many of readers wish to watch on video.

His essay is vivid like a child become an adult, but he is not childish at all, even he is matured with considering he is only 20 years old, and fairly bright.

Every child has his own strong vitality, but normally it will be exhausted on their grown up gradually.

As for him, he has not been spoilt much.not wilting

It is common type in Australian and European. So he is strong like a child.

If I add some words about his contents,

The meaning of WWOOF at Nudist is not good is only men in spa, same to public bath.

Going to Australia suspended School life!!

And good point is people over there so friendly and attractive as human.

But as for meal what he took,even not on the essay, He has been working at Japanese Restaurant 5 days a week.

But only 3 hours a day,He has enjoyed catering so much since eating as he wants at the restaurant,because the owner of the restaurant seems not managed restrictly.

I was there almost for eating,he said.

He called me two times.

One is when attacked by a burglar into his share house at Marlbour.

The other is when he wondered to go to Renmark from Adelaide with only 100$ with him.

Even all his friends stopped him, but he said I will go there,unless I go, I have no chance to know what happens, That is his strength.

~ From the introduction of APLaC (Association for Pluralistic life and culture) ~

Ahhh, no good I am shy.

So what I wrote there is shown on page 252.

If you may want to read original which on the web site, please access,,

Morishita Dai's English short course
You made it! → Well done!

Bondai Beach two day after arriving Australia.

stayed at BuckPacker in Sydney
for tow days（Tokyo Village）

Going to Australia suspended School life!!

At APLac office.
After working holiday.
Seems tough for me to write report and take video.

Mr.Tamura APLaC took
care of me so much!
Thank you!!!!!!

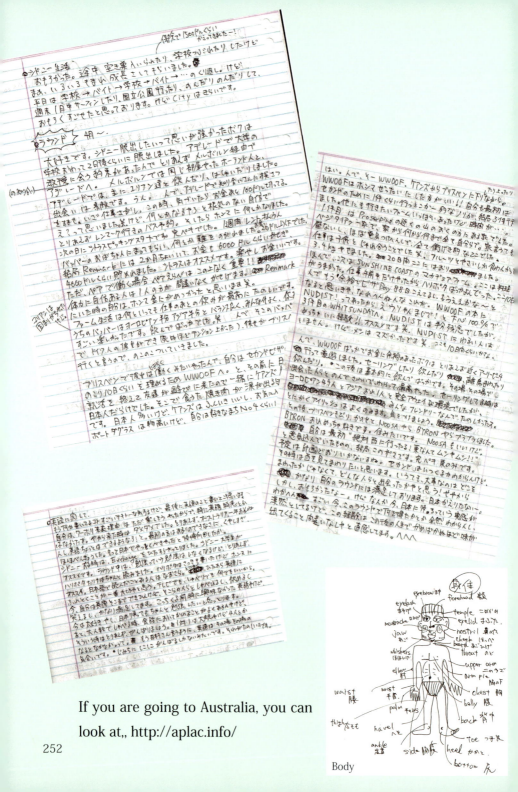

If you are going to Australia, you can look at,, http://aplac.info/

Life in Sydney
It was exciting.
Attacked by burglar(Covered about 1500$ by insurance),the English school has been bankrupt, through these experience I was grown up.

On week day, just repeating like as go to the school → working → school.
But on weekend,going to surfing all day,national park,and drinking.
So I think I have really enjoyed,but do not like the town..

Round April onwards
I have gone out Sydney just two days after the school finished

I had an appointment with the Professor at Adelaide,so I went to Adelaide via Melbourne.

At Melbourne,I had a chance to drink together with friends from poland,and at Adelaide I have enjoyed with with Korean friends.
Meeting someone is so nice. Yes,,
After I went to see the professor at Adelaide, then tried to find a job, at that time I found money only less than 100$,
I was surprised,but I thought I can manage with unfound confident, anyway booked bus for Renmark.
Amazingly It could get works from following day, Starting citrus picking.
It was perfect!

Asked aunt bapper to wait payment of rent fee for one week,I could manage it.
At that time I had only less than 20$..

Finally I have been staying at Renmark for about two months,earned about 6,000$ and could save 4,000$.
Citrus is recommended! Not so hard and good pay.
But In case work as a pair, selecting partner is so important!!
If you are confident enough with your physical fitness, you can earn more by yourself.
Working in Remark Farm,it is tremendous to drink together after work
My team(bapper) is consist 50% from Asian,and 50% is European,so good combination of races, good teamwork ,drinking together is so nice.(as for Korean,they are likely to be together by themselves)
I have gotton German girlfriend within the same team(Bapper).
It is so much excited (almost die).
Then I followed her when she went to Brisbane.

At Brisbane, she worked for the time being, so I have gone to WWOOF to get another
10 days for second visa.

Before then my friend came from Japan after finishing her recruitment activities went to Cairns together.
There were so many Japanese over there.

I was almost crying since grilled beef was so delicious over there.
Cairns is my favorite it has good atmosphere even so many Japanese,
Nearby there,Port Douglas should be No4 in my ranking even price is high.
Yes,talking about WWOOF,I went there from Cairns to Brisbane by detour.
I strongly recommend WWOOF!
Originally I had my plan to go only one for second VISA, but went 3 farms after all.
There were many farms where I would like to go, but no time.

First one was far end of the mountain near by Proserpine.
They are all vegetarian, make all from the house by themselves.
But as for the house,there no wall,no electricity at all.
It was shocking!

My job was just playing with children. smiling.
Eating only fruit and vegetable made me lose weight about 3 to 4 KG.
I have stayed there for twenty days.

Next is Academy farm in Sunshine Coast.
Meal was so nice there, and working the morning only, so I normally read Harry Potter in the afternoon. about 10 days been there.

So Already working day was more than 88days,I thought it will be enough.
But cannot be like this,,

Third one is at Whitsunday, WWOOF is nudist on the WWOOF guidebook.
so I went there with Ulterior motives 100%.
Nudist was half disappointed, but very good.it was good experience!!
Recommended Smiling
There were no bad people in Nudist ,even, meal over there was not nice,,smiling,,10days there too.

I went to Early beach near by the WWOOF,spent a much money since I haven't spent
Money at WWOOF.
Sailing, drinking, and islands tours, anyway after that, Just I have been keep drinking.

I had good time with people who just meet there occasionally.
Especially, When I had sailing, there were 49 Europeans and only one Asian,me.
I was absolutely away there,but everyone was very friendly,so I really enjoyed.

Irish people drink so much,Let's be careful of them.

Then After Returned back to Brisbaine,I travelled around Noosa,Byron with my girlfriend.

I love Byron, I would like to live there.Noosa also so good,,

Originally I wanted to go West,will ignore East! But as a result,east is all for me.
Plan is a just plan,never happen as I thought.
I don't know when I will be again as second VISA staying,wish to see west in next
time hopefully.

But Important thing is not where I go,should be what kind of people I meet.
So in this sense ,I am really satisfied with my round in Australia.
Do not want to back to Japan.
Really enjoyed here.
I do not realize I am going back to Japan now,and I am not sure what I have got by
This round,,But I am quite confident that this experience is how tasteful for my life towards future. Yeh,,,

Regarding with English
I am touching upon English although what I am writing up to here is just as I thought,,
The reason why I came to working holiday is just it seems so interesting not good at English.
So I was not good at all when I first arrived here.
Because Staying in Australia for one year,I should be good at English at least,,I thought,
But I have regretted many time not be prepared in Japan due to my poor English.
When I was in Sydney,I did Exchange all the time.
Recommends to do with students of the University of Sydney.

While rounding cannot have time to study,I have read Harry Potter.
Harry Potter is so recommended as I just touched now, especially for person who have
Read in Japanese already.
It seems very important to touch with English all the time via on TV,talk with someone.

I am satisfied with my English since I can talk,drink with somebody,laughing even my level
Is not so high.

I wish to continue to keep and learn English after back to Japan although I was not interested in English before came here.

And In case talking with large number of people.cannot catch up with conversation so often,Anyway shall we try to catch up!
One to One is no problem,but four persons makes difficult,,
In such a case,as Mr.Tamura said,Try your best from your bottom of heart.
There is no way unless trying to keep steadily.That is fun,too.

Extraordinary days for One Year

Extraordinary days for One Year
I am so much exciting since everything is new for me.
Make me consider a lot
Know thanks goodness for ordinal days.

    Ordinal days which have made me up to now.
    People whom I meet in extraordinary world.
    For them it is in ordinal days
    Like me,who is in extraordinary days.
    There are lives and ordinal days for each people.
    They will contact each other,
    It will Become my own experience.

Ask What I want to know
Since I know a little,
I have no chance to know more,
if closing within my own world.
Important to know measurement of thinking Direction to Osaka
in their own world.

    What is my world?
    University student, 21 years old.
    Okinawa Osaka and Working holiday.

Going to Australia suspended School life!!

Swimming, Water rock Rugby, and Lifeguard
Emily
Family and Friends
Archeology
Drinking
Vague

    What I want to get?
    What I want to do?
    I would like to keep smiling
    Better pleasant life
    Want a baby
    Make my parents happy
    Do not need to to do something special.
    Now fairly so happy.

Probably this year will become "the year" which.
I can meet quite large number of people,
and quite a different kind of people in my life.

I want to feel something from each of person who I meet with rather than knowing what they will get from me.

Good first impression People.
Potentially interesting people
Person who will be not get along with
Person can be friend immediately
All what I don't have
Expression is important
Really important
Be represented
It is likely to be hidden.

Dai In Australia

Since I will express myself,

    people will show more to me.

    Although thinking is important,
    not good to think too much.
    It makes more difficult

    Setting a goal day by day,want to keep fresh.

Anyway I really want to

    feel various happiness!!

Going to Australia suspended School life!!

Theory of feelings

It must be true,
Things which belong to girlfriend
looks so good somethig like that.

Plan is not always realized as planned

Plan is not realized all the time
as originally planned
Plan might be changed due to
meet someone.

28th Oct 2009 - 6th Sep 2010
April – Oct 2009 Sydney
April 2010 Start Rounding
Melbourne → Adelaide → Renmark(Two month in Citrus farm)
June Move to Brisbaine then after up & down on the east coast
Sep Sydney !!

10 months Already has been passed.
It seems happened yesterday, that I expected much for coming one year when I just arrived here.
Anyway so many things happened ,how can I write here?
I will write one by one based on what I did.

Map of Australia „Only this part going around in Australia.

Finding share mates at share house
At first time, everyone will be serious, but it will be interesting unexpectedly.
I have decided to share with after graduates of the University of Sydney since big size of
bed and good atmosphere of share mates after searching about 30 cases.
Let's enjoy finding share mate!
It is must be only occasion to go around in the city of Sydney.
After Sydney,I moved to Melbourne.Because of Surfing.

Myself now

I am interested in Maritime Archeology, but that's all.
Even I haven't started activities for looking for job yet, and don't know what I want to be.

But, now my life is so exciting, and not disappointed at all.
I really want to know how I can enjoy my life more.
One of the idea, going to graduate school.

Not just for enjoying,It must be more interesting to study Archeology hard.
It is meaningless to be worried that might be boring.
I have never known how exciting life saver is, before try it.

Once I will start something,I can get a opportunity to meet someone, and can grow up.
So I think it is worthwhile to start something new.

But In fact, This will be a big decision on my life, Studying at graduate School.
In addition, will try to get next step.

Searching in the sea.

Starting activities for looking for job and get a job or,
Cannot decide, in fact,, cannot decide,,

One year later,Two years later what am I doing? I cannot imagine at all, I am unstable,,

More choices makes me better,but too many choices.
I should feel how happy I am.

Still only I am 21 years old. I can do whatever I want to do.
Anyway it is good way to find out my direction by doing what I am interested.

So I will meet Mr.J.Kimura(*1) tomorrow,, and meet David(*2), too.
I wonder such a suffering guy can go to the world of Archeology,
Reach to the top, and survive,,,,,
It doesn't matter for me anymore.

It should not be any problem, even to fail, I would like to make my parents pleasure,
No! Parents are not concern.
I do not want to make my parents to excuse.

*1:Mr.J.Kimura is graduate from Tokai University Researcher in Australia. Wrote books on maritime archeology.
*2:David is Researcher of Archeology in Australia.
Introduced by Professor Araki as shown on Professor Ikeda's mail.
Dai did a rehearsal before meeting him.

How good if I can do what I want to do!

It is very difficult, but
this must be a good solution of feeling within myself.

    Yes,that is right,,
    Honestly, I think I wish to be shining.
    I would like to feel happy,,
    I would like to be a father, his children will be proud of him,
    Ohh, Life, yooo,,,,

Morishita Dai's English short course
It's itchy.   →   itchy !!

Going to Australia suspended School life!!

What I am interested in, now

Professor Ikeda is taking care of me so much.
→ It will be good opportunity for me.
I do not know this is my road or not,
So, I would like to know how Archeology' world is.

Maritime Archeology → I would like to meet Mr.Kimura

→ What do I ask him ?

- What Did he do in his graduate school? What is his major?
- What is a trigger to be interested in underwater?
- How? when he was in Japan.
- What is plan after graduate? Post Doctor?
   Life guard seems good for me,too.
- Not any other direction did he consider at all? (Probably yes)
- What is difficult thing?
- What is rewarding for you ?(absorbed)
- Did you suffer when you decide to go graduate school?(must be suffered)

From Dai Morishita
Sent 1st Feb 2010 10:22
To Jun Kimura
Subject Hello

Nice to meet you
My Name is Dai Morishita ,a student of 3rd grade of Archeology Laboratory
at University of the Ryukyus
I have got a introduction of you from Mr.David Nutley,so that I am sending my first mail to you.

Now I am staying in Australia with getting working holiday visa for one year.
As for my plan of staying Australia is studying at English conversation school at Sidney until the begging of March. then after going around Australia with working before going back to Okinawa at around September I am from Osaka originally,good at swimming ,love the sea.

Now I am interested Maritime Archaeology especially.

Last summer I have joined with the survey of Takashima by Professor E Ikeda as an assistant.

I am still a beginner of Archeology and I am wondering whether I can go ahead to Archeology for the future.
So I am sending this mail to give me a chance to meet with you if you may be convenient.

Now are you staying at Adelaide ?

Please permit me to send a sudden mail to you.

From Dai Morishita
Sent: Monday, 1 February 2010 10:22
To: Jun Kimura
Subject: こんにちは

はじめまして、
琉球大学考古学研究室3年次の森下（もりしたと申します。オーストラリアを回り9ヶ月になります。特技は水泳です。俺が大学に最近水中考古学に熱心的に興味を持ってきました。
令和、David Nutley 氏に木村さんを紹介していただき、メールさせてもらいました。

僕はワーキングホリデーでシドニーで大学して英語学校に行き、その後は後は大陸です。もちろん出身は大阪です。海も大好きです。
3月の調査では、シドニーに帰ろうと考えています。もちろん沖縄に帰ろうと考えています。
ところで沖縄に帰る前に、まだ自然のこ都合がよろしければ、ぜひ木村さんとお会いしたいです！

考古学に関してですが、池田榮史先生の調査の補助で鷹島の調査に参加してきました。
去年の夏には、池田榮史先生に関して、もし木村さんの都合がよろしければ、ぜひ木村さんとお会いしたいです。

今とても悩んでいます、もしよろしければアデレードでしょうか？？
木村さんの現在のお住まいはアデレードでしょうか？？

いきなりのメール失礼しました。

18／8／2010

Nationality is much related with their character, even we normally say that there is no concern with Nationality.

Japanese is Japanese.
Since I am in overseas now, I can find my own character more clearly.

Because all people around me are different nationality.

If I were in Japan,I suppose that difference of identity of each individual is weaker, since mind are similar.

Eventually Human is Human!!

With a kangaroo in Australia

Going to Australia suspended School life!!

20／8／2010　20：19

Ahh, I am feeling somehow
　　　　　　　　so happy now.
My life is really exciting.
I am a happy guy.

There are so many types of people in the world.
Meet someone is wonderful.

If I can become a man who can make full use of each meeting, It makes my life more excited.
It is really difficult, but I will try it.

In my mind, I am hearing "I'm yours"
　　　all the time, It is really nice song!

Emily

Now I am only one Asian among 44 people those who are european.
Amazing thing is how lucky we are that we could meet each other. To be honest, I do not feel european lady is so attractive, and they are not interest in Asia either.

I really think that we can fit each other, and really has got good opportunity reconsidering the way of watching peple,
thinking for Europe, and other many things by having chance to meet Emily.

Looking at my current situation, I think it is at most 10 % that I can come back Australia again in November next year.

I really wish to be with Emily from the bottom of my heart, but it is true that I would like to be back to Japan 90%, too.

There is no doubt that coming next year will make big impact on my life.
I wonder I should be in Japan or overseas, what kind of things I want to do.

Going to Australia suspended School life!!

I am really happy to meet Emily.
It is really sad for me to be
closer to the time
when I have to say bye to Emily.
At the end, I should put my life on
the stream, it is beyond my power.
Now I really wish to spend
my precious time as much as I can
Yes I wil do!!

i-Pod which I bought later,
There was a free service of
engraved mark on it.
I have wondered whether using
capital letter or small letter
Even one row or two row.
It is so important.

Then Finally I reached to this
sentence.

NO LADY NO LIFE

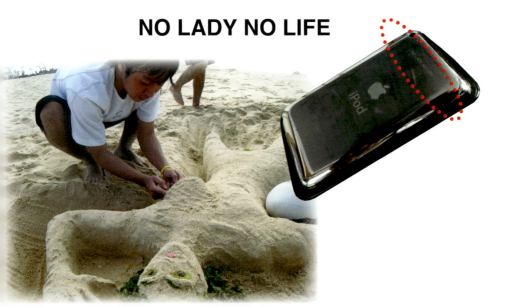

Back to Japan, and Return to my University of the Ryukyus!!

Hi, I have just came back from Australia!

Shall we meet someone who have not been met yet!!

I could have a chance to work as a lifeguard at Zamami Island same as last year after backing from Australia.
And return to my University, and swimming club, and Umi Bu.
In addition with this, newly joined with life saving club.
I have just settled down to get where to live after joining annual All Japan Water Rock Rugby Competition.,,,,(ˆ ˆ)

Everyday I am keeping to thank to many people after I came back to Japan.

Today I went to City hall to apply transference notification from overseas after two month since I came back to Okinawa.,

Then I was scold
'What did you do after coming, naughty boy!'
Thanks for scolding me, Ant

" Well,, It is just excuse to say I was so busy " „

So Coming Month January I will try „

Anyway I am in Okinawa now,
so shall we get along with all of you

Water Rock Rugby after one year ～☆

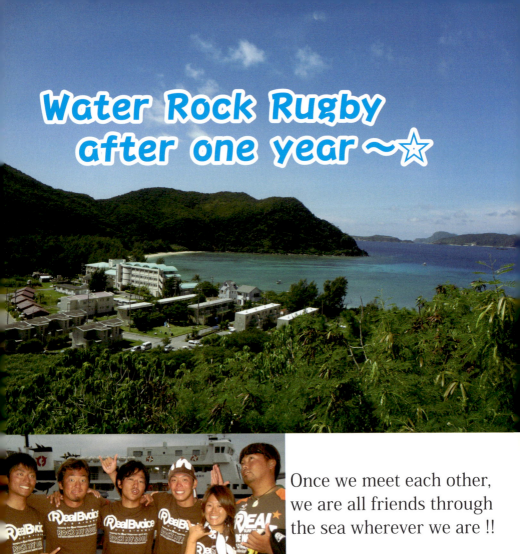

Once we meet each other, we are all friends through the sea wherever we are !!

My heavily used Parker

Chromis viridis in the clean Zamami's sea

Pools of swimming club of university of the Ryukyus.

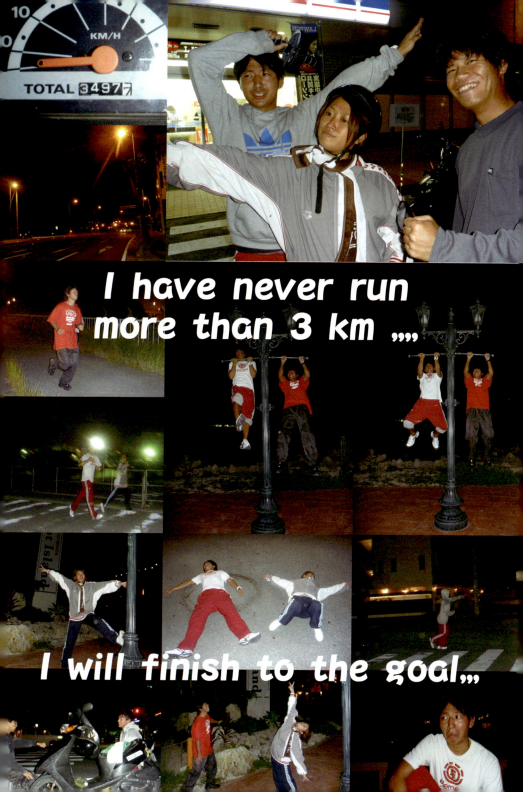

Finished Naha marathon with 4hours and a half!!
Going to public bath together !

Certificate of Finish 26th Naha Marathon

3630th Goal with 4hours 36min 00 second.

Certify your honor of Completion of Peace Memorial course(42,195km) At the 26th Naha Marathon.

5th Dec 2010

Takeshi Onaga Mayor of Naha City
President of Naha Marathon Association

Comment on the seminal note
6th Dec 2010
Yesterday,joined with Naha Marathon,and finished it,Wonderful!
Shall we entry by everyone in the next year!
I have pains on my legs due to running marathon.
Please assist me to become my legs,, Dai Morishita

Back to Japan, and Return to my University of the Ryukyus!!

TOEIC

To study TOEIC,
TOEIC is a just for getting job.
So it is important for me
to study now, try to score over
800 at least.

But TOEIC is not so important!
Try to study hard, and ready to
take examination!

That is important!
 I think something like this.

Current theme Get a job! or Graduate school!
2010.11.25

Self Analysis

Did my effort & Happy things	reason
Elementary School Playing with friends, Pokemon	Just make a fun
Junior High School Swimming, good friendship Thought I did my best	Since I have good friends who made Effort together wanted to finish through 3 years
High school Tennis Strong friendship But, regret to stop swimming meanwhile Love, That is all,	seems compare myself and others So often

University
1st Grade
  Swimming
 	
  Ichariba activities
 	
  Carrosan's
 	
  Firm friedship
	
	→ wanted to swim again
	
	→ So big impact having friends through Ichariba
	→ Just make a fun to start with,,,Eco circle
	Confident with happiness with in myself.

Back to Japan, and Return to my University of the Ryukyus!!

	Did so many things as I wanted. Enjoy the meeting with various people
University 2nd Grade Archeology	→ struggled more tough than I thought Almost giving up which not capable for me once,
Life saver	→ Don't know trigger to start it Maybe biggest change on my college life, A, I, U, E, O So comfortable in the sea, People there so nice Nature is so good,, Everybody here has high motivation. Meeting with good person
University 3rd Grade Australia	→ Seems fantastic Kick off to Australia since thought to be worthwhile based on my experience in Okinawa Really important one year Become interested in English Recognized how tough to earn money by working

Read through Harry Potter,,,

Human is Human wherever they live.
Friend who can get along with doesn't matter where come from.
Money also important

Friend is fortune!!

Human can do almost all,once they have a will to do.

Don't hesitate before you do!

I really wish to enjoy my life

Want to meet people from various countries.

Family is precious

Would like to know more about Japan

Would like to work in Japan

Would like to know more

Would like to be attractive person

Would like to be Innocent

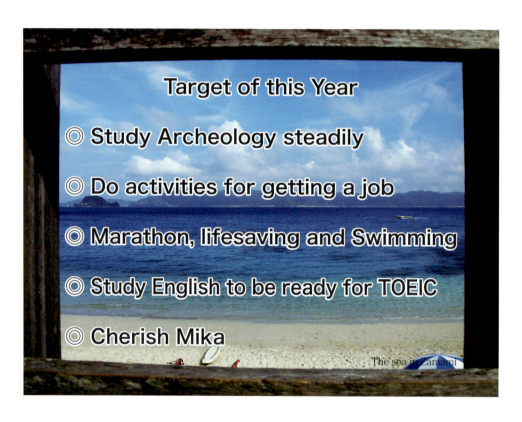

What is enjoying life?

Keeping own hope enhancing enjoying present time!!

Do not consider too much!!

Present

Extending my root deeper and deeper

Well, Put the pen here!!

Dai Morishita
『 curriculum vitae
of 21years old 』

Dai Morishita 『curriculum vitae of 21years old』

History of Dai Morishita

22nd Feb 1989		Born in Cardiff City South Glamorgan County Wales United Kingdom
Sep 1991	2Years Old	Kindergarten Roath Park Cardiff
24th July 1992	3Years Old	Back to Japan
April 1993	4Years Old	Ibaraki Municipal Ibaraki kindergarten(Middle Grade)
31st July 1994	5Years Old	Move to Kuala Lumpur Malaysia
Sep 1994		Kindergarten of Japanese School of Kuala Lumpur Malaysia
April 1995	6Years Old	Primary School of Japanese School of Kuala Lumpur Malaysia
30th Mar 1998	9Years Old	Back to Japan
April 1998		Move into Ibaraki Municipal Oike Primary School
Mar 2001	12Years Old	Graduate Ibaraki Municipal Oike Primary School
April 2001		Ibaraki Municipal Higashi Junior High School (Swimming Club)
Mar 2004	15Years Old	Graduate Ibaraki Municipal Higashi Junior High School
April 2004		Enter Osaka Prefectural Settsu High School (Tennis Club)
Mar 2007	18Years Old	Graduate Osaka Prefectural Settsu High School
April 2007		Enter National University of the Ryukyus Faculty of Law and Literature Human Sciences Course (Swimming Club)
		Meet Water Rock Rugby and Lifesaving
Oct 2009	20Years Old	temporary absence from University
		Stay Australia as Working Holiday
Sep 2010	21Years Old	Back to Japan
		Back to University
18th Dec 2010		Passed away by accident at Ginowan City Okinawa

Buddhist name Shaku Tai Kai(Ocean)

考古学研究方法論 II
Archaeological research methodology II

世界の水中遺跡の調査

提出日：2009/2/6（金）

Archaeological research methodology II
Investigation of underwater ruins of the world

法文学部人間科学部二年次
071828K

森下　大

Submit on 6th Feb 2009(Fri)
Faculty of Law and Literature Human
Sciences Course 2nd Grade
071828K

Dai Morishita

はじめに

　第二次世界大戦後、水中機器の発達により水中遺跡調査の活動が盛んになった。1960年代は、水中考古学が新しい学問専門領域の確立をめざし、学史的にもその存在理由の問われる10年間であった。1970年代においては、世界各国で水中に関する関心が高まり、アメリカの大学では、学科の新設も起こった。世界各国では水中遺跡に関わる研究機関が地域的枠を超えて国際的研究活動を推進し、水中遺跡調査の学際的協力体制の充実を図り続けている。そして1980年代は、水中考古学の実践の10年間となった。本レポートでは、1980～89年に世界中において、調査が行われた水中遺跡についての分類、分布について見ていく。

外国における水中調査

Refer on Page after next.
↓

Comment
(1) 沈船
(2) 船に関する遺物
(3) 港湾都市とそれに伴う遺物
(#1)~(3)のカテゴリに含まれない遺構、遺物
いずれかの化、不明

　以上の図は、世界の水中遺跡調査分類と地域別件数分布図（図1）である。この図では、A,アメリカ大陸地域、B,ヨーロッパ地域、C,地中海地域、D,アフリカ地域、E,オセアニア地域、F,アジア地域に地域分類をしている。図から、どのような地域でどのような水中遺跡の調査が行われたのかが伺える。どの地域においても、主な水中遺物は沈船、または船に関わる遺物であることがわかるだろう。また調査件数も地域によって大きな差があることがわかる。

　ここからは、各地域での水中考古の現状についてさらに詳しく見ていこうと思う。

と、社会の関心度が増大し市民たちの協力があった。だが、一方ではいかに水中文化財を保護メリカ）、レッドベイ海底ラセリトス遺跡（メキシ

ンマークやノルウェーと心が強い。フランスは、に水中調査を行っている行われてきた。そのためら残っている。また、イ事によって指定された遺跡交館など、興味深いものが

遺跡（セイシェル諸島）、サ

ック海底遺跡（フランス）、遺跡（イギリス）など

C,地中海地域
　地中海地域は分布図でみてもわかるように、世界の中でももっとも水中調査が行われている地域である。地中海はその海を取り巻く環境から、水中考古学を新しい専門領域の学問としてすすめていく上で重要な役割を果たした。

遺跡例：
青銅器時代海底遺跡（トルコ南部）、ファラサルナ港湾都市遺跡（クレタ島）、ジアルディニナクソス海底遺跡（シシリー島）など

D,アフリカ地域
　アフリカでは水中遺跡の調査は調査数から見て、あまり行われていないようである。調査四件のうちの半分の二件はオランダ東インド会社の船であった。

遺跡例：

るため、17世紀前半からーストラリア政府は沈没船しい水中遺跡を発見し、国が払われた。海底の文化財ことがさらにオーストラリ

春（オーストラリア）、トー

比べるとまだ浅い。本格的である。日本では、江差町沖

ア）、グリフィン号沈船海

　本レポートをとおして、世界でどのような水中遺跡の調査を知ることができた。この分布は1980年代のものなので、その以後、水中遺跡の調査がどのように変化したかということも勉強しようと思う。そして私自身、水中遺跡の調査に関わってみたいと強く感じた。

参考文献
1999　『遺跡保存方法の検討―水中遺跡―』　文化庁文化財保護部記念物課

Archaeological research methodology II
Investigation of underwater ruins of the world

Submit on 6th Feb 2009(Fri)

Faculty of Law and Literature Human Sciences Course 2nd Grade

071828K

Dai Morishita

Introduction

After World War II Activities of Underwater ruins investigation have been flourished due to Development of underwater equipment.

In 1960's It is a decade for searching Reason for existence of Academic History aiming establishment of academic disciplines of Maritime Archeology.

In 1970's Increased interest on the water around the world,and have been stablished New department at University in US.

It is going to continue efforts to enhance academic cooperation by that world research institutions involved in water ruins to promote international research activities beyond the regional framework in various countries in the world.

Then in 1980's it became the decade of practice on the Maritime Archaeology. In this report I will describe regarding with classification and distribution of surveys of underwater ruins in 1980 to 1990.

Chart 1 Surveys of underwater remains for overseas countries

Above map shows classification and geographical distribution map of the world

by underwater ruins surveys.(Chart1)

On this chart it is divided into following regions such as

A:Americas region,B:European regions,C: Mediterranean region,

D:African Region,E:Oceania region,F:Asian region.

In any area from the figure, the main underwater ruins we'll find to be a relic involved in wreck or ship.

In addition,we can find out big difference on number of surveys among regions.

From now on, I will look at in more detail for current conditions of maritime archaeological in each region.

Comment

(1)Wreck

(2)Ruins of Ships related

(3)Harbor city and its related ruins

(4)Ruins not related with (1) to (3)

(5)Others,unknown

A:Americas region

In 1980's interest for underwater ruins in the society has been increased. Not only specialists of underwater remains,but also Abandoned Shipwreck Act has been enforced in addition with cooperation by citizen.

On the other hand, Stolen of Underwater cultural heritage by mateur divers has become a problem.

So It is quite important to protect underwater cultural heritage.

Example of Remains

Whydah Underwater remains(US), Mississippi river bed ruins(US), Red Bay Underwater remains(Canada), Port Royal Underwater remains(Jamaica), Isla Mujeres(Mexico)

B. European Region

There are many variation on maritime Archeology in European countries

High interest in the remains of Viking era of ship with their history in North Europe like Denmark and Norway.

France has made great contribution on development of equipment for underwater survey after world War Ⅱ.

In Dutchland,Reclamation have been made for expansion of land since lands is lower than sea level,so there are some records of discovery of ancient shipwrecks around the seabed by reclamation work.

In United Kingdom, Protection of Wrecks Acts has been enforced in 1973,

Remains which have been specified by the law has reached to the number of 34. There are many interesting remains such as Wreck owned by the East India Company

Example of Remains
Tingstrade Trask Underwater remains(Sweden), Aber Wrac'h underwater remains(France)
Mary Rose underwater remains(UK), Amstordam underwater remains(UK)

C: Mediterranean region
Mediterranean region is most active region on underwater surveys as you can see the map of surveys.
Mediterranean has made great role on progress of maritime Archeology as new specialty of academic with the environment of surrounding the sea.

Example of Remains
Underwater remains of Bronze age(Southern Part of Turkey)
Phalasarna Port town remains(Greece Crete Island)
Giardini Naxos Underwater remains(Italy Sicily Island)

D. African Region
It seems not active judging from the number of surveys
The number of surveys is 4,two cases are the ship owned by Vereenigde

Oostindische Compagnie.

Example Remains

The Mauritius Underwater Remains(Gabon Republic)
Boudouso Underwater Remains(Seychelles Islands)
The Santo Antonio de Tanna Underwater Remains(Kenya)

E. Oceania Region

In Western Australia coastal areas,coral reefs and shoals are developed, there are Records of wreck since first half of 17the century.

Australian Government has enforced Historic Shipwrecks Act for protecting those wrecks.

In addition, on this law, the person who discover a new underwater ruins and report to the country will be given reward.

In fact the person who have found it got the reward.

Personal interest and understanding for the cultural assets of underwater remains is returned as reward.

This support the enlightenment activities at Australian society in general

Example of remains
The Tryal Underwater remains(Australia)
The Pandora Underwater remains(Australia)
The Taupo Underwater remains(Newzealand)

F. Asian Region

The history of Underwater remains in Asia is new compared with Europe and Medeterranean.

Asian countries have started their full scale surveys almost same time at First half of 1970's.

In Japan,The Kaiyo maru underwater remains at Esashi town is the first.

Example remains

Pttaya Underwater Remains(Thailand)

Jambuair Underwater Remains(Indonesia)

The Griffin Underwater Remains(The Philippines)

Xin'an Underwater Remains(Korea)

At the end,

I could find various surveys of Underwater remains all around the world through this report.

This chart shows at 1980's.so I would like to study further surveys of underwater remains
After that.

And I myself would like to involve to survey of underwater remains.

Bibliography

Study of Determination of ruins preservation method Underwater remains (Agency for Cultural Affairs Cultural Properties Protection Division Monuments Dept.

SPECIAL THANKS!!

Thanks for your cooperation with introducing many stories, giving precious photos, documents for making this book.

Without your support, this book never been established. In really It must be introduced all of your name here, please be patient to show photos in stead.

Thank you my friends!

(From the left)   **Professor Mr.Eishi Ikeda**
University of the Ryukyus Faculty of Law and Literature of
Human Sciences Department of Archaeology Laboratory

Associate Professor Mr.Masahiko Goto
University of the Ryukyus Faculty of Law and Literature of
Human Sciences Department of Archaeology Laboratory

Professor Mr.Shozo Nakamura
University of the Ryukyus Assistant to the President
Advisor of Life Saving Club

Mr.Taishi Otono
Chairman NPO Okinawa Water Patrol System

Mr.Akira Otsuji (Occhi san)
Director Okinawa Lifesaving Association(OLA)

Ms.Chiyomi Mizutani
Teacher Osaka Prefectural Settsu High School (In charge classroom at 3rd Grade)

Mr.Katsuyoshi Toyoda
Representative NPO Waterwise

Mr.Yoshiyuki Awa(Kampachi san)
Member of Team Legend Water Rock Rugby

Mr.Shouei Okabe
Japan Surfball Association

Thank you for having time to meet me, even so many friends not taking photos,,

Keep moving regardless of happiness.

Keep Going.

Thanks for meeting everyone!!

Lifesaver Dai at Zamami Island

What is Ohana ?

It pronounce OHANA（恩波仲）meaning Family with writing OHANA in Hawaii.
Water man who love the sea,they call Ohana each other hoping with sharing strong will of heavy(will) Word(Soul) and will(Stone)
Fellow who continue to trust each other toward the same purpose
"Favor（恩）" which received from predecessors
"Wave（波）" continue to pass to next without any expectation

Will which respect nature and sea　Sincerity keep believing fellow.
"Fellow（仲）", T shirt made by the occasion of All Japan Water Rock Rugby every year.
There is Ohana word printed on back of T shirt, 9th All Japan Water Rock Rugby competion at Tokashiki Island November 2011.

Mr.Toyoda shared with everyone
with saying that Dai（大）is
in the middle of Favor（恩）.

Yes,I am with all of you
all the time from now on.

All get from experiences!

DAI MORISHITA